THE RAINHILL TRIALS

ANTHONY DAWSON

First published 2018

Amberley Publishing
The Hill, Stroud,
Gloucestershire, GL5 4EP

www.amberley-books.com

Copyright © Anthony Dawson, 2018

The right of Anthony Dawson to be identified as the Author
of this work has been asserted in accordance with the
Copyrights, Designs and Patents Act 1988.

All rights reserved. No part of this book may be reprinted
or reproduced or utilised in any form or by any electronic,
mechanical or other means, now known or hereafter invented,
including photocopying and recording, or in any information
storage or retrieval system, without the permission in writing
from the Publishers.

ISBN: 978 1 4456 6975 5 (print)
ISBN: 978 1 4456 6976 2 (ebook)

British Library Cataloguing in Publication Data.
A catalogue record for this book is available from the British Library.

Typeset in 10pt on 13pt Celeste.
Typesetting by Amberley Publishing.
Printed in the UK.

Contents

	Foreword	4
	Acknowledgements	5
Chapter 1	Why the Rainhill Trials?	6
Chapter 2	A Novel Approach	22
Chapter 3	Unparalleled	37
Chapter 4	The *Rocket*	54
Chapter 5	After Rainhill	76
Chapter 6	Conclusion	87
	Bibliography	94

Foreword

Writing this foreword in my Shildon office, I am feet away from the original *Sans Pareil*, half a mile from the site where it was constructed, and elsewhere in the Locomotion museum today, Jane Hackworth Young is working with a team of volunteers on cataloguing and listing historic documents. Therefore I might be accused of bias in writing, but having also worked at the Museum of Science & Industry in Manchester and also currently being Senior Curator of Rail Transport & Technology at the National Railway Museum (with *Rocket* and *Sans Pareil* in my care), I think I can plead a level-headed approach. Having worked on both replica locomotives too, I have a practical insight in part to what went on in 1829 as well, so was delighted when Anthony asked me to write the foreword for this book.

The story of the Rainhill Trials is very much like the book of Genesis in the Bible. It's a familiar tale, known by many but not always understood as it should be. The parallels are clear: both events are all about beginnings, and when one begins to analyse them, deeper stories and meanings become clear with ramifications throughout the centuries to come.

Anthony Dawson has managed to distil and meld historical documents, eye witness reports and twentieth-century comment and research into a readable account of the eventful days in the autumn of 1829. His words are not the first to be published about the Trials, nor are they perhaps the most lengthy – but in terms of accessibility, readability and setting the whole event in context, this is the record that melds engineering and social history in a way that will please enthusiast and layman. There is much to learn from his research and writing, I know I certainly have, and I commend the book to you.

Anthony Coulls
Shildon, 23 January 2018

Acknowledgements

As is traditional at this point in a book, I should like to thank all those involved in the writing and production of it. Firstly, to Andy Mason for his proof-reading and technical drawings as well innumerable cups of tea, shoulder to cry on and continued support of my literary endeavours. To all the Railway Volunteers (past and present) at MOSI in Manchester for their encouragement, and especially Matthew Jackson for his technical input; Danielle Bryers for checking the manuscript and Jordan Leeds for his input on steam boilers. To David Boydell, Matthew Jackson and Lauren Gradwell for use of their personal photographs; and finally, to Anthony Coulls for his foreword.

Unless credited, all photographs are by the author or are from the author's collection.

Chapter 1

Why the Rainhill Trials?

The Rainhill Trials, held between 6 and 14 October 1829, were instigated by the directors of the Liverpool & Manchester Railway to find the best motive power for their as-yet unopened line. The trials were the result of a report by James Walker (1781–1862) and John Urpeth Rastrick (1780–1856) comparing the merits – or lack thereof – of locomotive haulage and fixed engines. Walker had carried out the first survey of the Liverpool & Manchester Railway, while Rastrick had been in business first as Hazeldine & Rastrick (they built Richard Trevithick's (1771–1833) *Catch Me Who Can* in 1808) and later, as Foster, Rastrick & Co., manufactured early locomotives including *Agenoria* and *Stourbridge Lion*. Walker and Rastrick had cautiously concluded in favour of stationary engines and rope haulage; tellingly, however, Walker had concluded that the locomotive engine was capable of great improvement, while the stationary engine was already a mature technology.

Built by Foster, Rastrick & Co. of Stourbridge in 1829, the *Agenoria*, a contemporary of *Rocket*, demonstrates the final evolution of the 'self-propelled beam engine' type of locomotive. She worked at the Shutt End Colliery until *c.* 1865 and was presented to the Science Museum in 1885.

The steam locomotive in 1828 was still a very crude self-propelled kettle. Walker and Rastrick toured the North East and visited short colliery lines, such as the Middleton Railway in Leeds, where locomotives had been in use since 1812. Even here, Blenkinsop's patent locomotives only operated on level stretches of track, with winding engines being used to haul the coal wagons up inclined planes. On the Stockton & Darlington, locomotives were used in conjunction with winding engines and horses. In 1828 that railway was suffering from a motive power crisis. The four Stephenson locomotives, like others of the period, were designed for short colliery lines, not a lengthy 25-mile (40 km) run. They were often short of steam – despite the gradient being in favour of loaded trains heading to Stockton – and their fires clinkered easily, something confirmed by experimental data gained from the *Locomotion* replica.

Timothy Hackworth (1786–1850) was the 'Superintendent of the Permanent and Locomotive Engines' on the Stockton & Darlington Railway from May 1825 – a position he enjoyed due to the recommendation of George Stephenson (1781–1848) – with an annual salary of £150 and 'the company to find a house, and pay for his house, rent and fire'. It was his job to keep the locomotives and fixed plant in working order and eventually he became the running superintendent, keeping the trains moving too. For a brief period in 1824 he was works manager at the Forth Street Works of Robert Stephenson & Co. where, together

Full-size working replica of George Stephenson's *Locomotion No. 1*. *Locomotion* was one of four similar locomotives built for the Stockton & Darlington Railway. (Lauren Jaye Gradwell)

with James Kennedy (1797–1886)[1], he would have supervised the construction of the first Stephenson locomotives for the Stockton & Darlington.

These four locomotives were small, four-coupled engines with an inefficient single flue passing through the boiler, most of the combustion products escaping straight up the chimney and doing little useful work. Furthermore, the large-diameter flue impeded circulation of water in the boiler, so that while the top of the boiler would be scorching hot, the bottom would be cold to the touch. To get the best out of these engines, their drivers often tied down their balance-weight safety valves, and did so at the risk of their own lives: *Active No. 1* exploded on 1 July 1828, killing her driver, John Cree, after he had tied down her safety valve. *Active* was rebuilt and pressed back into service. Elsewhere, on the Hetton Colliery Railway, the Stephenson-built locomotives were withdrawn from service on part of that line and replaced by fixed engines. Back on the Stockton & Darlington, operating costs spiralled and shares plummeted: an anxious George Stephenson wrote to Hackworth in July 1828 asking him whether the rumour about 'lay[ing] off the Locomotive Engines' was true or not.

Despite the Liverpool & Manchester Railway Prospectus of May 1824 noting the use of steam locomotives, the directors were divided in their opinion over locomotives and stationary engines; Secretary and Treasurer Henry Booth (1789–1869) was an enthusiastic supporter, while James Cropper (1773–1840), for example, was decidedly against, and had a personal dislike towards Messrs Stephenson. He would later become a vocal champion of John Braithwaite (1797–1870) and John Ericsson (1803–1889). On 29 September 1828 the directors, on account of

> The various and contradictory accounts which prevailed with respect to the power and relative economy of Locomotive Engines ... as compared with Horses ... considered desirable that one or two of the Directors, accompanied by the Treasurer should proceed to Darlington to ascertain as correctly as practicable the results of the experience of that line. [RAIL 371/1]

This deputation reported back a month later, in favour of stationary engines: given the poor performance of these early locomotives it is easy to see why. George Stephenson was an ardent supporter of the locomotive from its very earliest years. He wrote a furious reply, arguing that stationary engines required more capital outlay than the equivalent number of locomotives; that the ropes were dangerous, more prone to accidents, especially where crossing public roads; and finally, that if one locomotive failed, traffic could continue, but if one stationary engine were to fail, the whole line would be paralysed until that engine could be repaired. He informed the directors that experiments were 'now in progress' for 'ascertaining the practicability of burning coke' by locomotives. Stephenson further argued that locomotives were more flexible operationally, and it was cheaper to purchase additional locomotives to cope with an increase in traffic rather than additional stationary plant. After digesting this report,

---

1 After leaving Stephenson's employ he became a partner with Edward Bury as Bury, Curtis & Kennedy of Liverpool. Bury and Kennedy had hoped to enter their *Dreadnought* at Rainhill but it was not finished in time.

Above and below: The original *Locomotion No. 1* (although powered by a petrol engine in the tender) was the star of the Stockton & Darlington Railway Centenary in 1925 – hauling a train of chaldron waggons, and proceeded by a rider with a red warning flag.

9

the directors met on 6 November 1828. Lithographic copies of Stephenson's report were circulated and at the suggestion of James Cropper, Henry Booth was instructed to discuss the relative merits of stationary engines with Benjamin Thompson of the Brunton & Shields Railway: Thompson, like Cropper, however, was biased in favour of stationary engines and rope haulage. Booth duly reported at the meeting of 17 November the results of this inquiry in favour of rope haulage, but the directors were still divided over the choice of motive power. As a result they commissioned Walker and Rastrick to carry out their thorough fact-finding mission during the winter of 1828/29.

The poor performance of the early locomotives encountered by Walker and Rastrick led them to conclude that they could not climb hills (and, where employed, would have needed stationary engines with ropes to help them up) and were restricted to running on the level, or down a favourable gradient. The capital out-lay to work the line using locomotives was calculated at £90,963 14s 3d, nearly £10,000 cheaper than by using stationary engines and ropes, but the latter, however, were more economical in day-to-day operation. Thus, to Walker and Rastrick, the steam locomotive of 1828 appeared to be unpredictable and dangerous, and rope haulage by fixed engine appeared to be the safer, cheaper and more reliable alternative. Walker and Rastrick reported the same to the Board of the Liverpool & Manchester on 9 March 1829. In reply, Robert Stephenson (1803–1859) and Joseph Locke (1805–1860) published their response a month later, repudiating many of the claims of Walker and Rastrick, especially that regarding the hill-climbing ability of locomotives. Robert wrote, 'Locomotives shall not be cowardly given up. *I will fight for them until the last. They are worthy of a conflict.*'

Stephenson even sought Hackworth's counsel because at that time it looked, in Hackworth's words, like the Liverpool & Manchester was going to be 'strangled by ropes':

New Shildon, April 9 1829

I am verily convinced, that a swift Engine upon a well conditioned Railway, will combine profit – simplicity and, will afford such facility, as has hitherto been known ...

My general opinion, as to the L M System. I believe, it, is in a comparitive state of infancy – swift Engines upon a double way I am convinced, may be used, to the utmost advantage – improvements, upon anything yet produced of greater importance, in all respects, are clearly practicable, & I am sure this will prove itself, by actual remuneration to such parties as prudently yet diligently pursue the execution of this kind of power ...

Stationary Engines, are by no means adapted to a public line of Railway. I take here no account of a great waste of Capital, but you will fail in proving to the satisfaction of any one not conversant with these subjects, the inexpediency of such a system- it never can do for coaching – passengers cannot be accomodated – if endless ropes are used, there will be both danger, and delay. [NRM Hack 1-1-22]

Hackworth concluded by telling Stephenson to hold firm in his belief in the locomotive:

I hear the Liverpool CO. have concluded to use fixed Engines. Some will look on with surprise; but as you can well afford it, it is all for the good of the science, & the trade, to try both plans. Do not discompose yourself, my dear Sir, if you express your manly, firm

Right and below: Chapman & Buddle's *Steam Elephant* of *c.* 1815. This operable replica was completed at Beamish in 2001 and gives a good impression of the type of locomotive encountered by Rastrick and Walker as they made their survey. (Lauren Jaye Gradwell)

decided opinion, you have done your part, as there adviser. And, if it happen to be read someday in the newspaper——whereas the Liverpool & Manchester Railway – has been strangled by ropes, we shall not accuse you of guilt in being accessary either before or after the fact. [NRM Hack 1-1-22]

In his report, however, James Walker had made the optimistic suggestion of offering a premium for 'the most improved' steam locomotive:

> To enable you to take advantage of improvements which might be made (in steam locomotion); with a view to encourage which, and to draw the attention of Engine makers to the subject, something in the way of a premium, or an assurance or preference, might be held to the person whose Engine should, upon experience, be found to answer the Best. The Rainhill (stationary) Engines would at the same time enable you to judge of the comparative advantages of the two systems. [Walker & Rastrick: 29-30]

Thus, on 20 April 1829 the directors of the Liverpool & Manchester Railway resolved to offer a premium of £500 for the

> Locomotive Engine, which shall be a decided improvement on those now in use, as respects to the consumption of smoke, increased speed, adequate power, & moderate weight. [RAIL 371/1]

Steam Elephant and a short train of appropriate rolling stock, depicting the Stockton & Darlington Railway in the 1820s. (Lauren Jaye Gradwell)

It was not just the motive power of the Liverpool & Manchester Railway that was at stake, but rather the future of the steam locomotive itself. The successful locomotive at Rainhill would set the mould for the railway locomotive for decades to come. But moreover, if the locomotive were found to be a failure at Rainhill, then the development of not only the locomotive but also railways as whole would have been affected. Thus, Rainhill became a defining moment in history.

The 'Grand Mechanical Competition'

The Directors resolved that the trial would be held on a mile and a half stretch of completed railway, 9 miles east of Liverpool, called Rainhill. The 'stipulations and conditions' of the Rainhill Trials were issued on 25 April 1829, containing many lessons learned from the study of the operation of early locomotives, including the use of springs; two safety valves (including one which was 'tamper proof'); an effective pressure gauge; and the pressure-testing of boilers to prevent explosions. The stipulations were drawn up by a group of directors including James Cropper, Joseph Sanders, William Rotherham, Robert Benson and John Moss. George Stephenson as their engineer probably had some input, too. Thus, the design criteria for the entrants for the Trials were:

A later French depiction of the Concours de Rainhill; while the depiction of *Rocket* (centre) is fairly accurate, the other locomotives are less precise.

1st. – The said Engine must 'effectually consume its own smoke,' according to the provision of the Rail-way Act, 7th Geo. IV.

2nd. – The engine, if it weighs Six Tons, must be capable of drawing after it, day by day, on a well-constructed Rail-way on a level plane, a Train of Carriages of the gross weight of Twenty Tons, including the Tender and Water tank, at the rate of Ten Miles per Hour, with a pressure of steam in the boiler not exceeding 50lb. on the square inch.

3rd. – There must be two Safety Valves, one of which must be completely out of the reach and control of the Engine-man, and neither which must be fastened down while the Engine is working.

4th. – The Engine and Boiler must be supported on Springs, and rest on Six Wheels; the height, from the ground to the top of the Chimney, must not exceed Fifteen Feet.

5th. – The weight of the Machine, *with its complement of water* in the Boiler, must, at most, not exceed Six Tons; and a Machine of less weight will be preferred if it draw after it a *proportionate* weight; and if the weight of the Engine, &c., do not exceed *Five Tons*, then the gross weight to be drawn need not exceed Fifteen Tons; and in that proportion for Machines of still smaller weight – provided that the Engine, &c. shall still be on six wheels, unless the weight (as above) be reduced to Four Tons and a Half, or under, in which case the Boiler, &c. may be placed upon four wheels. And the Company shall be at liberty to put the Boiler, Fire Tube, Cylinders, &c. to the test of a pressure of water not exceeding 150lb per square inch, without being answerable for any damage the Machine may receive in consequence.

6th. – There must be a Mercurial Gauge affixed to the Machine, with Index Rod, shewing the Steam Pressure above 45 pounds per square inch; and constructed to blow out at a Pressure of 60 pounds per inch.

7th. – The Engine to be delivered Complete for trial, at the Liverpool end of the Rail-way, not later than the 1st of October next.

8th. – The price of the Engine, which may be accepted, not to exceed £550 delivered on the Rail-way; and any engine not approved to be taken back by the Owner.

N.B. – The Rail-way Company will provide the *Engine Tender* with a supply of Water and Fuel for the experiment. The distance within the Rails is four feet eight inches and a half.

Henry Booth notes that the directors were inundated with submissions from engineers and members of the public alike:

> Multifarious schemes were proposed ... from all classes of persons ... all were zealous in their proffers of assistance; England, America, and Continental Europe were alike tributary ... The friction of the carriages was to be reduced so low that a silken thread

Thomas Shaw Brandreth's entry, *Cycloped*: quite literally a two horse-power machine.

would draw them ... Hydrogen gas and high pressure steam – columns of water and columns of mercury – a hundred atmospheres at a perfect vacuum – machines working in a circle without fire or steam, generating power at one end of the process and giving it away at the other ... Every scheme which the restless ingenuity or prolific imagination of man could devise was liberally offered to the Company: the difficulty was to chose and decide. [Booth: 69]

Of these 'multifarious schemes', five locomotives were eventually chosen: Robert Stephenson and Henry Booth's *Rocket*; Timothy Hackworth's *Sans Pareil*; John Braithwaite and John Ericsson's *Novelty*; Timothy Burstall's (1776–1860) *Perseverance*; and the *Cycloped* by Thomas Shaw Brandreth (1788–1873). *Perseverance* was sadly damaged en route, but when she did steam failed to meet the minimum trial stipulations and Burstall was awarded £25 in aid of his expenses. Ross Winans's (1796–1873) hand-cranked 'manumotive' and Brandreth's horse-powered *Cycloped* were certainly the most unusual entrants. Although often considered a joke, John Rastrick's notebook reveals *Cycloped* was taken seriously (if, perhaps, only by him). He notes *Cycloped* was worked by two horses on a treadmill, geared down using small wheels 11.5 inches in diameter to work the 40-inch driving wheels. Rastrick calculated *Cycloped* was capable of at least 10 mph with the horses walking at 3 mph. The *Mechanics' Magazine* (31 October 1829) described *Cycloped* to its readership:

The motive-power in this engine is gained in the same way as in tread-mills of prison celebrity ... only of horses, instead of men ... are employed ... A common waggon-frame

15

mounted on wheels is divided longitudinally into two compartments or stalls, and the bottom of these stalls is occupied by an endless chain of cross-bars, which work into and revolve around the carriage axles [there was gearing between the tread-mill and driving wheels]. The horses are placed in the stalls, and by treading on the endless chains produce the rotary motion requisite to propel the carriage forward.

The apparatus was of rude construction, and can scarcely be said to have given the principle of the invention fair play. The stalls, in particular, were too narrow, and greatly cramped the action of the horses. We have no doubt that in a well-constructed carriage of this description, horses might be made to work on a railway with considerably more effect than drawing, or, at least with equal effect and more ease.

The Judges

Three judges were appointed: John Urpeth Rastrick of Stourbridge (whom we've already met), Nicholas Wood (1795–1865) of Killingworth Colliery and John Kennedy esq. (1769–1855) of Manchester. Wood was an advocate of the locomotive and a close friend and ally of George Stephenson; Robert (1803–59) was apprenticed to him. In his obituary, Wood is described as: 'Of commanding height, portly form, and had a ruddy, good-humoured countenance, which bore no traces of the hard work he got through.'

Both Rastrick and Wood had considerable experience of both railways and locomotives; Wood had carried out experiments on the resistance of rail-borne vehicles, and between horse and locomotive power in 1818, including the study of the form and durability of rails – work which was carried out in conjunction with George Stephenson. He published his famous *Treatise on Railroads* in 1825. Kennedy was one of the founders of the Liverpool & Manchester Railway. He was a wealthy Unitarian millwright (i.e. mill machine maker) and cotton spinner who traded as McConnel[2] & Kennedy. McConnel & Kennedy's mill in Ancoats was among the first steam-powered mills in Manchester and one of the largest in the world. Kennedy's background in engineering and machine making – Rastrick had also been apprenticed as a millwright – would have stood him in good stead alongside his colleagues.

The Rainhill Trials

In order to inspect the site of the Rainhill Trials, the directors and three judges visited Rainhill on 5 October 1829, in a train of 'blue carriages' drawn by *Rocket*:

> From Huyton, in cars drawn by Mr Stephenson's locomotive, which moved up the incline plane from thence with Great Velocity. They were accompanied by many scientific gentlemen whose presence was hailed with numerous cheers. [*Gore's Liverpool Advertiser*, 8 October 1829]

---

2 The McConnels, too, have played their part in railway history: William McConnel (son of James, Kennedy's business partner) opened the Tal-y-Llyn railway to serve his slate quarry in North Wales.

Rocket, Sans Pareil and *Novelty* as depicted (to the same scale) by the *Mechanics' Magazine* in October 1829.

The judges made a 'formal inspection' of the course (which had been surveyed by Rastrick) and of the locomotives entered for the Trial. By ascending the Whiston Inclined Plane drawing her train of carriages, *Rocket* had indirectly nullified the Rainhill Trials by showing that a locomotive could draw a useful load up hill.

The first day of the Trials was on Tuesday 6 October 1829, held before a 'vast concourse' of spectators; the *Liverpool Mercury* estimated at least 10,000 persons were present. The directors, each wearing a white ribbon on their hat or lapel, arrived in a train of 'blue coaches' drawn by *Rocket*, perhaps showing their official favour to their Engineer

(George Stephenson) and Treasurer (Henry Booth). The *Liverpool Courier* (7 October 1829) opined that:

> Never, perhaps, on any previous occasion, were so many scientific and practical engineers collected together on one spot as there were on the Rail-Road yesterday. The interesting and important nature of the experiments to be tried had drawn them from all parts of the Kingdom, to be present at this contest of Locomotive Carriages, as well as to witness an exhibition whose results may alter the whole system of our existing internal communications.

According to the *Manchester Mercury*, the 'locomotive carriages ... attracted the attention of every individual on the ground' and during the morning

> Ran up and down the road ... more for amusement than experiment, surprising and even startling the unscientific beholders by the amazing velocity by which they moved along the rails. Mr Robert Stephenson's carriage, attracted the most attention during the early part of the afternoon. It ran, without any weight being attached to it, at the rate of *twenty-four miles in the hour*, shooting past the spectators with amazing velocity, and emitting very little smoke, but dropping red-hot cinders as it proceeded. [*Manchester Mercury*, 13 October 1829]

Charles Blacker Vignoles (1793–1875), fierce rival of George Stephenson and co-patentee with Braithwaite and Ericsson, provided much of the 'copy' for the *Mechanics' Magazine*. It is not surprising, therefore, that the *Mechanics' Magazine* was biased against the Stephensons and a vocal champion of *Novelty* and her builders, even after it had become abundantly clear that she was a technological dead end. Furthermore, the *Mechanics' Magazine* was a London publication, for professional, learned men: pretty much the same group of London experts who had first disbelieved and then belittled George Stephenson's invention of the miner's safety lamp in 1816 and claimed he could never cross Chat Moss. Not only did the Stephensons and Booth have to contend with the London 'establishment' being set against them, but because most provincial newspapers took their copy for the Rainhill Trials verbatim from the *Mechanics' Magazine*, or the equally anti-Stephenson *Liverpool Mercury*, national opinion via the press was set against them.

It was natural, therefore, that Vignoles via the *Mechanics' Magazine* belittled *Rocket*'s achievements; she had only reached 18 miles per hour, but with 'A great inequality in its velocity' and, contrary to the Stipulations, made smoke. By suggesting *Rocket* was making smoke, Vignoles was insinuating that *Rocket* should have been disqualified, leaving the way open for *Novelty*. Henry Booth notes that while *Rocket* did make smoke, it was because some coal had been mixed in with the coke and the mistake was soon rectified. The Trials proper began that afternoon, and *Rocket* was the first on trial:

> Cars containing stones were then attached to it, weighing, together with its own weight, upwards of 17 tons, preparatory to the trial of its speed being held. The precise distance between the point of starting, at or near the weighing shed, to the point of returning was 1 ¾ mile, four times forward and four times back, equal to 14 miles in the space of

75 minutes, exclusive of stoppages; but including the stoppages the average rate of speed, with a load augmented by passengers to 13 tons, was full 15 miles an hour. [*Manchester Mercury*, 13 October 1829]

Unsurprisingly, Vignoles thought *Rocket*'s performance 'just exceed[ed] the stipulated minimum' and, while many of the spectators had thought it 'surprising enough', thus far they had seen 'nothing to contrast it with': that contrast would come from *Novelty*.

Following the experiments with *Rocket*, Braithwaite and Ericsson's *Novelty* was next placed on trial; from her compactness and neat appearance, the *Liverpool Mercury* thought her 'the beau-ideal of a locomotive engine'. John Dixon (1795–1865) thought because she was 'all covered with copper like a new Tea Urn,' *Novelty* had a 'very Parlour like appearance'. The *Mechanics' Magazine* sang her praises:

> The great lightness of this engine, (it is about half lighter than Mr. Stephenson's) its compactness, and its beautiful workmanship, excited universal admiration; a sentiment speedily changed into perfect wonder, by its truly marvellous performances. It was resolved, first, to try its speed merely ... that is at the fastest rate at which it would go ... it darted off at the amazing velocity of twenty-eight miles an hour! Had the railway been completed, the engine would ... have gone nearly the whole way from Liverpool to Manchester within the hour; and Mr Braithwaite has, indeed, publicly offered to stake a thousand pounds, that as soon as the road is opened, he will perform the entire distance in that time. [*Mechanics' Magazine*, 10 October 1829]

The *Manchester Mercury* continued:

> Its performance, when exercising without a load, was most astonishing, passing over 2¾ miles in seven minutes and a quarter, including a stoppage. With this delay, its speed was about 23 miles an hour. While running, the progress was upwards of 28 miles an hour. Owing to a variety of circumstances, the engine was prevented from being ready to start with a load until a late hour, when, at the request of the Directors, its exhibition was postponed until the Wednesday [7 October]. [*Manchester Mercury*, 13 October 1829]

The *Liverpool Chronicle* noted 'the total performance of the engine within the hour averaged 27¾ miles', achieving 'the unprecedented and almost incredible' speed of 32 mph; the *Liverpool Mercury* estimated her fastest speed at a more realistic 28 mph. The *Chronicle* noted that locomotives like *Novelty* would soon be able to run between Liverpool and Manchester, which were then 'half a day's distant', within the hour.

Novelty was prepared for running on the morning of Wednesday 7 October. The *Mechanics' Magazine* notes that 'with a load of three times its own weight attached to it, or 11 tons 5 cwt', *Novelty* managed a maximum speed of 20¾ miles per hour, 'proving itself to be equally good for speed as for power.' One eye-witness thought 'it actually made you giddy to look at it.' The *Manchester Mercury* opined that:

> We hear some prejudice has arisen reflecting on its strength and duration of its speed ... At all events, this is the first locomotive engine these gentlemen ever constructed, and it

was four months after the appearance of the advertisement offering the premium that they first thought of applying the principle of their patent boiler to generate locomotion on a rail-way ... It was only on the first of August that it was put in hand ... and on the 28th September arrived by the canal at Liverpool! ... Mr Stephenson has been making locomotive engines for many years; that he has been more especially contemplated bringing forward a locomotive engine for a rail-way; that he knows well the effect, and is well accustomed to travel such engines along a rail-road; and that more especially ... he had had more opportunities for exercising his engine. [*Manchester Mercury*, 13 October 1829]

Vignoles added 'We took particular notice ... of its power of consuming its own smoke' – he had been at pains to observe that *Rocket* made smoke, and how *Novelty* was the quietest of the locomotives at Rainhill. This latter point surely has to be fiction as *Novelty*'s cylinders exhaust directly to the atmosphere; the replica can be heard puffing away 5 minutes before it can be seen and travels shrouded in a cloud of exhausted steam. But something was wrong; the blowing mechanism, so vital to the performance of *Novelty*, broke down ('from an explosion of inflammable gas which burst her bellows'), which meant that her formal trial was postponed. This was the first of several mechanical failures that led to *Novelty* being withdrawn from the Trials. The *Mechanics' Magazine* conveniently ignored this breakdown, and instead noted:

The weather now became wet, and the rail-ways clogged with mud, which made it necessary to suspend the execution of the experiments before the day had half elapsed.

This suspension of the Trials allowed Rastrick, Wood and Kennedy to meet to discuss the stipulations of the Trials. Speed alone was not going to prove which locomotive was going to be the most efficient machine day-in, day-out, hauling passenger trains from Liverpool to Manchester. It was clear that the existing rules, issued back in April, had to be modified to take this into account: with the railway still not complete throughout, the only way to observe how the engines would perform over the distance from Liverpool to Manchester and back (70 miles) was over the short 1¾-mile course at Rainhill. The amount of coke and water consumed was to be measured, to ascertain which locomotive not only was the most effective but most efficient.

Thus, on the morning of Thursday 8 October printed cards bearing the new 'Stipulations and Conditions' were issued.

The Weight of the Locomotive, with its full compliment of water in the boiler shall be ascertained at the weighing machine, by eight o'clock in the morning, and the load assigned to it shall be three times the weight thereof. The water in the boiler shall be cold, and there shall be no fuel in the fire-place. As much fuel shall be weighed, and as much water shall be measured and delivered into the tender-carriage, as the owner of the engine may consider sufficient for the supply of the engine for a journey of thirty-five miles. The fire in the boiler shall then be lighted, and the quantity of fuel consumed for getting up the steam shall be determined, and the time noted.

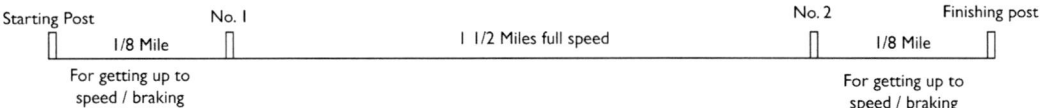

The Rainhill course. (Andrew Mason after John Rastrick)

The Tender-Carriage, with the fuel and water, shall be considered to be, and taken as a part of the load assigned to the Engine.

Those engines that carry their own fuel and water, shall be allowed a proportionate deduction from their load, according to the weight of the engine.

The engine, with the carriages attached to it, shall be run by hand up to the starting-post; and as soon as the steam is got up to fifty pounds per square inch, the engine shall set out upon its journey.

The distance the Engine shall perform each trip, shall be one mile and three-quarters each way, including one-eighth of a mile at each end for getting up the speed, and for stopping the train; by this means the engine with its load will travel one mile and a half each way at full speed.

The engine shall make ten trips, which will be equal to a journey of thirty-five miles; thirty miles whereof shall be performed at full speed, and the average rate of travelling shall not be less than ten miles per hour.

As soon as the engine has performed this task, (which will be equivalent to the travelling from Liverpool to Manchester), there shall be a fresh supply of fuel and water delivered to her; and as soon as she can be got ready to set out again, shall go up to the starting-post, and make ten more trips, which will be equal to the journey from Manchester back to Liverpool.

The time of performing every trip shall be accurately noted, as well as the time occupied in getting ready to set out on the second journey.

Should the engine not be enabled to take along with it sufficient fuel and water for the journey of ten trips, the time occupied in taking in a fresh supply of fuel and water shall be considered and taken as part of the time in performing the journey.

The judges were also granted additional powers by the directors:

10 Oct. 1829. Resolved: That Messrs. Rastrick, Kennedy & Wood or any two of them have full powers to fix the mode, and limit the period of the Trial of the Locomotive Engines now competing for the Prize. Charles Lawrence, Chairman. [NRO.602/15]

The *Mechanics' Magazine* howled with rage; the 'marvels' performed by (the albeit crippled) *Novelty* were all to naught. It also noted that the clause of 'effectually consuming its own smoke' appeared to have been quietly dropped – perhaps, it suggested, because *Rocket* had only 'partially fulfil[ed]' that clause.

21

Chapter 2

A Novel Approach

Braithwaite & Ericsson of London had only learned about the Rainhill Trials and its premium of £500 seven weeks before the trials were to commence. John Braithwaite was the third son of John Braithwaite the elder (1760–1818), the inventor of the Diving Bell. Braithwaite junior was a talented engineer, inheriting his father's business in 1818, and was

Full-size replica of Braithwaite & Ericsson's *Novelty*, built by the Science Museum in 1929, incorporating all four original wheels, the original left-hand cylinder and various motion components. (Matthew Jackson)

introduced to George and Robert Stephenson in 1827, the same year he became acquainted with Swedish army officer John Ericsson. Braithwaite's younger brother, Frederick (1798–1865), trading as Braithwaite, Milner & Co. of London, later built locomotives for the Eastern Counties Railway and exported fourteen to the USA.

Novelty was very much the establishment locomotive: she had been built in London, and John Braithwaite was very much part of the London engineering establishment, unlike the two Northern, chapel-going, self-taught engine-wrights Stephenson and Hackworth. Invariably described as the 'people's choice' by the biased *Mechanics' Magazine* and its allies, she was the 'right choice' by the 'right sort' of people. The 'upstart' Stephensons were not 'the right sort' of people.

Ericsson came from a noted engineering background: his father Olaf Ericsson (1778–1818) was involved in building the Göta Canal while his older brother Nils Ericsson (1802–70) was a noted canal and railway engineer. After the talent of the brothers had been spotted by Count Baltzar von Platen (the architect of the Göta Canal), both were enrolled in the Swedish Navy as 'cadet mechanics'. John and Nils were subsequently commissioned into the Swedish Army: John to the Jämtland Rifle Regiment (resigning in 1830 with the rank of captain) and Nils in the Engineers, later transferring to the Navy Mechanical Corps, retiring in 1850 as a colonel. In 1826 John obtained three years' leave from the Army and travelled to London, forming a partnership with John Braithwaite.

As Braithwaite & Ericsson, they built some of the earliest, if not the first, steam-driven fire engines. Their first essay – sharing its name with the later locomotive, *Novelty* – was built in 1829 and used a highly efficient boiler designed, and later patented, by Braithwaite,

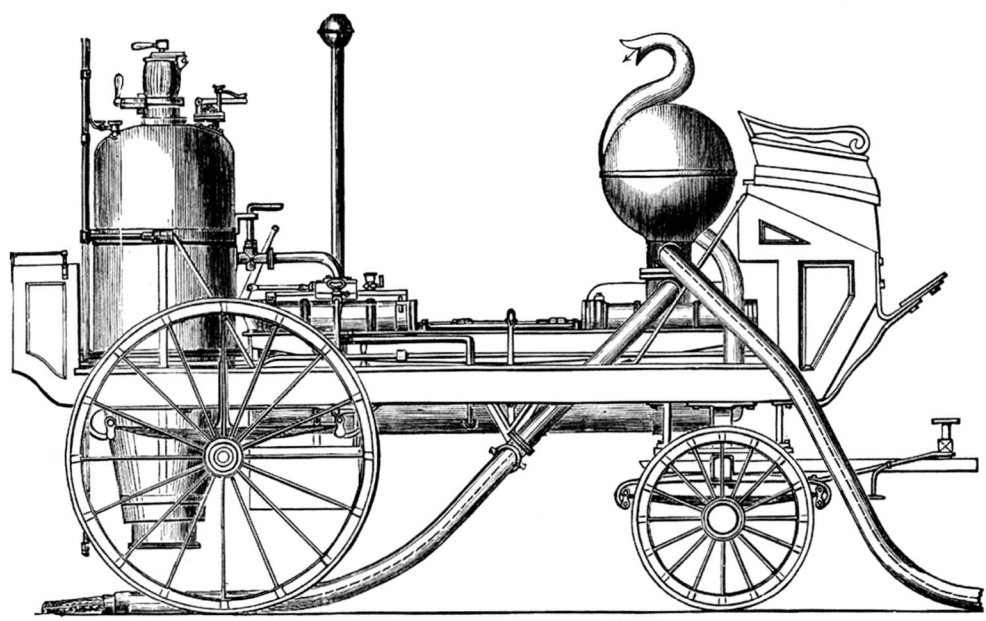

FIRST STEAM FIRE-ENGINE EVER BUILT—LONDON, 1829.
The "Novelty," George Braithwaite, Builder.

Braithwaite & Ericsson's steam fire-pump *Novelty*, completed in 1829. Notice the similarity with the locomotive of the same name.

Ericsson and Vignoles. This first fire engine was used to great success fighting a fire at the Argyll Rooms in London, managing to pump 30 tons of water an hour. It had two cylinders, 7 x 16 inches, producing 10 hp. It was carried, like its locomotive namesake, on wheels designed and patented by Theodore Jones of London in 1826. Given the short space of time Braithwaite & Ericsson had to build the locomotive *Novelty*, and the similarity in design, it is easy to wonder how much of the fire engine *Novelty* was simply re-purposed as the locomotive *Novelty*.

They sold their third fire engine to the Mersey Docks & Harbour Board in 1831. It had twin horizontal cylinders working a crankshaft, developed 15 hp, and cost £1,200. Their fourth engine, *Comet*, was built in 1832 for the King of Prussia, with horizontal cylinders 12 x 14 inches, and the boiler was pressed to 70 psi. A fifth, experimental, engine was built in 1833. Unfortunately for Braithwaite and Ericsson, the London Fire Engine Establishment was opposed to steam-driven fire pumps on land, believing that there was insufficient water for them. They had no problems with water-borne steam pumps, however, and one was duly built in 1835 by Braithwaite and Ericsson, using the same boiler technology as *Novelty*, the engine being able to drive the paddle wheels or the pumps.

Raising Steam

The key to the success of any steam-powered machinery is its ability to raise and maintain steam pressure. Braithwaite and Ericsson did so in an entirely novel way, using a two-part boiler with a horizontal water-filled section containing a copper flue tube and a vertical element containing the fire (surrounded by water) at its base and forming a steam space at the top. Vignoles provided uncritical details about *Novelty* to J. C. Robertson, editor and publisher of the *Mechanics' Magazine* (who was also present at Rainhill):

> The Furnace is supplied with fuel from the hopper, through the vertical tube in the centre of the steam-chamber; the heated air from this furnace passes off through a flue, which is made to wind twice or thrice up and down the [horizontal] cylinder, and gradually diminishes in diameter till its termination in the escape pipe.
>
> The extent of the surface exposed to the action of the heat ... is a great deal less than in other engines ... but instead of depending on the atmospheric draught ... make[s] use of the bellows-sort of apparatus ... to force the air through the fire; and by thus supplying a greater quantity of caloric in a given time, they obtain an effect precisely analogous to what would result from doubling or quadrupling the size of the furnace and the extent of its flue. Nor is that all: the quantity of atmospheric air which is introduced under the fire ... has not only the effect of forcing the heated air onwards through the flue, but is itself a source of heat – equivalent to the employment of so much additional coke. It is in these two circumstances – the acceleration of the draught and the supply of fuel (if we may so speak) derived from the atmosphere – that the great merit of "The Novelty" – the secret of its vast superiority – consists ... It can generate a greater quantity of steam in a given time than was ever before produced by an apparatus of equal capacity. [*Mechanics' Magazine*, 24 October 1829]

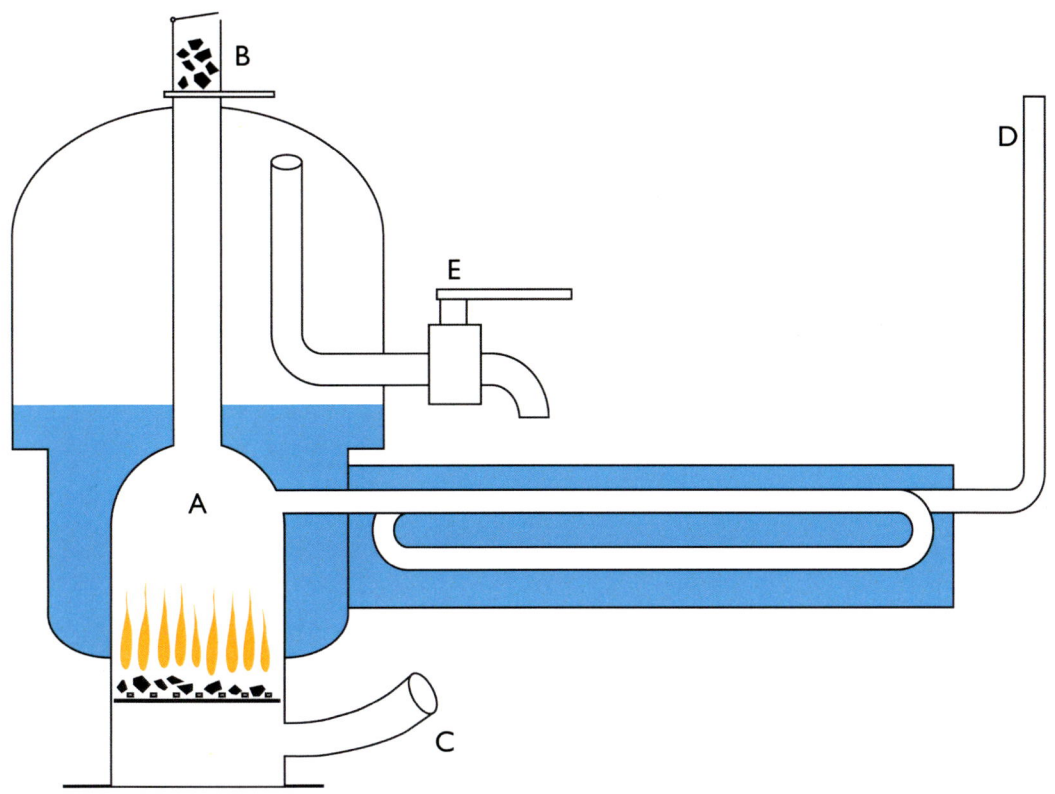

The boiler of *Novelty*, showing the firebox (A); coke hopper (B); bellows-pipe (C); flue tube terminating in the chimney (D); steam riser and regulator (E). (Andrew Mason after John Rastrick)

Not everyone was impressed with the rhetoric of Vignoles and Robertson. The editor of the *Register of Arts* concluded that:

> "The Novelty" ... does not appear to us to possess, in its essential parts, much of that character which its name indicates; however its general appearance may differ from the ugly tea-pot forms of those generally used in the coal districts ... Now, we cannot for the life of us discover any thing about this "Novelty" that is not common to other locomotives, except the steam-producing apparatus; and this apparatus, considered distinctly from the carriage, has but little *Novelty* – it has been used in France, "time out of mind" for heating baths; and in England under endless modifications for evaporation generally. [*Register of the Arts*, Vol. IV (1830)]

While Braithwaite and Ericsson's boiler might look unusual, it essentially consists of an upright cylindrical firebox surmounted by a steam dome, with a horizontal boiler barrel with a flue tube passing through it. By passing hot air through a long, narrow, S-shaped boiler flue in the horizontal section, it was working in the same way as the multiple short flues in the boiler of *Rocket* (Chapter 4). By tapering the tube from entrance to exit – just like the U-shaped flue of *Sans Pareil* (Chapter 3) – Braithwaite

25

and Ericsson hoped to increase the pressure and therefore speed with which the hot gasses moved through the flue tube, improving its heat transfer characteristics. Unlike *Rocket* or *Sans Pareil*, *Novelty* used a forced draught, rather like *Lancashire Witch* of 1828 (Chapter 4) or the locomotives of Marc Séguin in France (Chapter 4). This was using existing technology and ideas from the blast furnace or smithing hearth to get a coke fire to burn as hot as possible. Furthermore, by providing large quantities of air through the base of the fire, Braithwaite and Ericsson hoped that this would lead to the coke fuel burning efficiently and without smoke. Coke is mostly pure carbon, produced by heating coal in a retort to drive off the volatile gasses (hydrogen, oxygen and sulphur). These gasses were usually collected and sold as 'town gas'. Because the volatiles – which, when incompletely burned, cause smoke – have been driven off, coke is a relatively smoke-free fuel. It does, however, require a lot of air to burn efficiently. The blowing apparatus – a variation of George Vaughan's patent blower of 1826 – was driven by eccentrics on the leading axle of the locomotive and was designed to provide a constant flow of air through the fire. According to their patent, there were 'cocks to regulate the transmission of air' into the fire grate from the blower, controlling the air flow and therefore burn characteristics.

The 1979 working replica of *Novelty*, built by Flying Scotsman Enterprises, running at MOSI during 'Riot of Steam', held to mark the 175th anniversary of the Liverpool & Manchester Railway in September 2005. (David Boydell)

Dropping *Novelty*'s fire: it was found difficult to manage the fire, which was prone to clinkering. The flue tube also quickly became blocked with carbon. (David Boydell)

The vertical extension of the firebox, leading to the hopper at the top, worked as a combustion chamber – i.e. an extension to the firebox which increases the combustion space, and time, thus increasing the fuel efficiency of the boiler. Therefore, it would also have been filled with hot gases, contributing in part to heating the water but primarily drying the steam in the 'steam chamber', which surrounded it.

There were several weak points in the design: the first was the joint between the vertical and horizontal sections of the boiler. The second was effective fire management. Because the boiler had to be kept air-tight there was no traditional fire-hole door so the fireman could inspect the fire. Instead, coke was loaded into a hopper at the top of the boiler and then let down into the firebox below by means of a trap-door. There was no way of telling how well the fire was burning, whether it was too thick, or if it had started to clinker: the replica suffered badly from clinker, and when the fire was dropped, a solid, circular sheet of clinker was removed. Finally, there was no way of cleaning the serpentine flue which passed through the horizontal section of the boiler. The replica of *Novelty* suffered from the flue tube becoming progressively blocked, and impeding performance, during the Rainhill re-enactment in 2002: the only way to remove the blockage was to dismantle the boiler.

Boiler Problems

Unfortunately for Braithwaite and Ericsson, their patent boiler was found to infringe an existing patent of Thomas Cochrane, 10th Earl of Dundonald (1775–1860) and Alexander Galloway (1776–1847) of May 1818. Cochrane, a naval hero who had been cashiered in 1814 and then served in the Greek, Brazilian and Chilean navies, had an inventive mind, patenting a tunnelling shield used by Marc Brunel (1769–1849) during the digging of the Thames Tunnel; he designed steam ships in the 1820s and a rotary steam engine during the 1830s – one of which was tested on *Rocket*.

This infringement resulted in a lengthy and expensive four-year legal case. In June 1830, Cochrane and Galloway went to the Court of Chancery to demand an injunction against Braithwaite and Ericsson. Braithwaite's patent stated that his boiler was an air-tight system, using a forced draught of air to encourage the fire to burn and to force the hot gases through the flue tube and thence exhaust. Cochrane and Galloway's boiler was similar, but the crucial difference was that they used a spring-loaded valve on the exhaust to prevent the hot air escaping, the 'air thus being retained within the furnace and flue'. By the use of such a valve the heated air was prevented from escaping from the system. To prevent smoke, the exhaust was bubbled through a column of water.

Marc Brunel was called as an expert witness by Cochrane and Galloway, and he attested 'that the defendants [Braithwaite and Ericsson] have committed an important and glaring infringement'. In reply, Braithwaite and Ericsson wheeled out their own 'big gun': Richard Trevithick, who 'carefully examined' both patents and found that there were crucial differences between the two designs, with Braithwaite and Ericsson's boiler, unlike Cochrane's, relying on the 'free passage of air through the boiler', passing 'through small flues at a great speed'. Furthermore, while Braithwaite and Ericsson's patent had been taken out in January 1829, over a decade after that of Cochrane and Galloway, it was found that the latter's boiler 'was, in point of fact, not in use until one year after Mr Braithwaite's patent was obtained'. Although in July 1830 the Lord Chancellor threw out an injunction

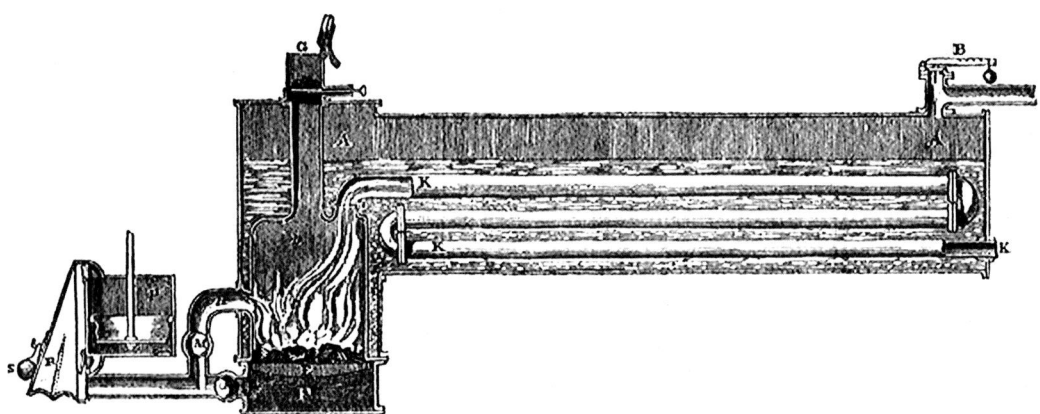

John Braithwaite's patent boiler of 1829 which caused him so much legal trouble: the similarities with *Novelty*'s boiler are apparent, including the upright firebox, S-shaped flue tube and bellows to liven the fire.

against Braithwaite and Ericsson, the case rumbled on and they ultimately lost their case in 1834, and were forced to pay damages to Cochrane and Galloway.

In theory *Novelty*'s was an excellent boiler design. Davidson and Glitheroe (2006) concluded that *Novelty*'s boiler was the most efficient of the three main competitors at Rainhill, with 'very good heat transfer characteristics'. How *Novelty* would use that steam and perform under trial, however, was a different matter entirely.

Using the steam

Novelty was powered by a pair of pedestal-mounted cylinders at her front (blowing apparatus) end, 6 x 12 inches, which John Rastrick calculated would produce 5.74 hp. Davidson & Glitheroe, however, put this figure slightly higher at 6 hp. The cylinders worked downwards and, because the locomotive was mounted on springs, acted on bell-cranks which in turn worked connecting rods driving a cranked axle: the first use of a cranked driving axle on any locomotive. Often described as an 0-4-0, *Novelty* was in fact a 2-2-0, the driving axle being positioned immediately in front of the firebox. Nicholas Wood suggests that *Novelty*'s wheels could in fact be coupled with chains as required, although whether this feature was ever used at Rainhill is unknown. Certainly John Rastrick does not mention it in his notes, and the *Mechanics' Magazine* is silent on the matter.

The valve gear on *Novelty* was far cruder than on *Rocket* or *Sans Pareil*: her valves were operated by eccentrics on the driving axle, mounted between the crank throws and the axle boxes. Long, diagonal eccentric rods ran forwards to a rocking shaft mounted under the

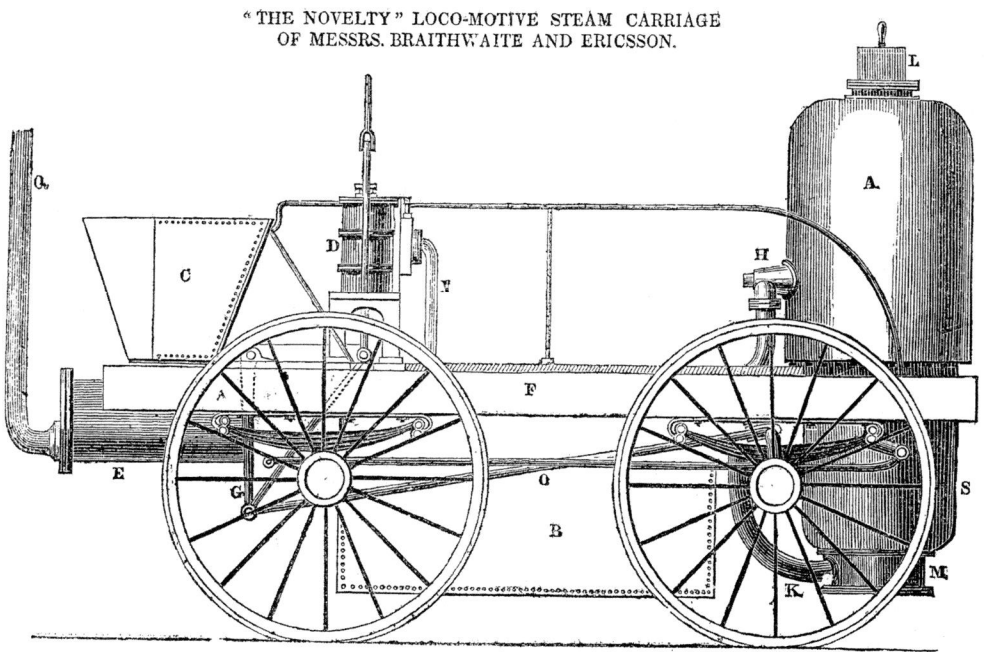

Novelty as drawn by the *Mechanics' Magazine* in October 1829. Key features include the upright firebox (A), water tank (B), blower (C), cylinders (D), horizontal boiler barrel (E) and exhaust (F).

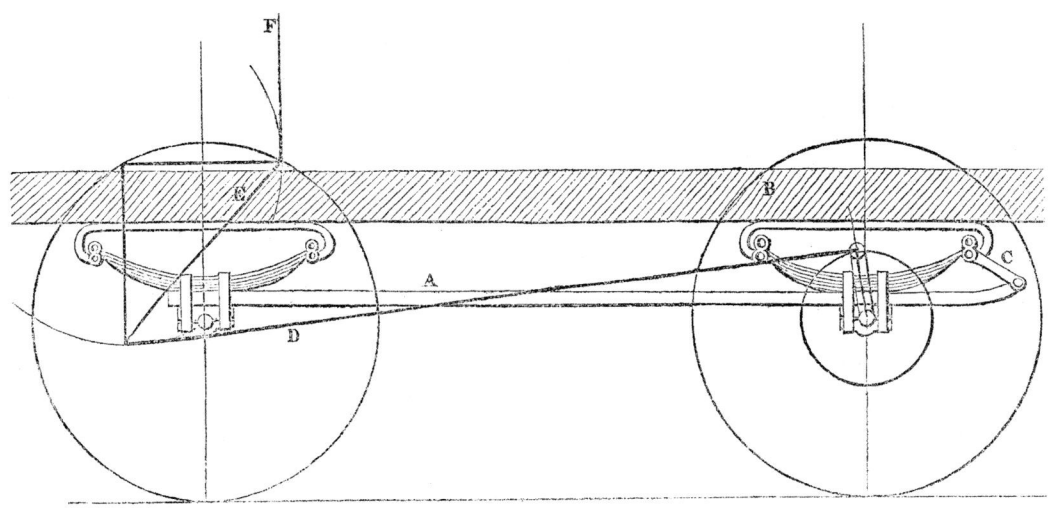

Novelty's final drive was from the vertical cylinders (F) working a bell-crank with a fixed-pivot (E) which drove the connecting-rod (D) working the cranked axle.

platform, level with the rear of the cylinder pedestals, which worked gab-ended levers. The gabs hooked over pins on the valve handles, which worked the valves. To change direction, the locomotive had to be brought to a dead stand and the gabs manually unhooked from the pins. Unlike the other two entrants, direction could not be changed on the move; nor could back-pressure in the cylinders be used as a brake.

Novelty's 51-inch (1.29 m) diameter wheels were of an all-metal construction, formed from a wrought-iron hoop, with fourteen 1-inch (25 mm) diameter iron spokes off-set around the hub like those of a bicycle. Braithwaite and Ericsson had used this design of wheel before on their steam fire-engines. All four original wheels survive and were incorporated into a non-working replica of the *Novelty* built by the Science Museum in 1929. The *Mechanics' Magazine* was of the opinion that:

> The wheels are of the excellent description patented by Messrs. Jones and Co., and the choice of them by Messrs. Braithwaite and Ericsson is as strong a tribute as could have been paid to their merits. From the peculiar manner of their construction they act with the least possible interference from the weight of the engine, and being perfectly cylindrical [unlike early cast iron wheels], bear equally with their whole breadth on the rails. The lightness for which the wheels are famed, is not in this instance so remarkable ... Of the total weight of 2 tons 15 cwt., we believe 18 cwt. Falls to the share of the wheels.
> [*Mechanics' Magazine*, 17 October 1829]

Not only was *Novelty* the first locomotive to use a crank axle, she was the first tank engine, carrying 122 imperial gallons of water – far less than her competitors – in an iron well tank slung under the frames. This had the advantage of lowering the centre of gravity, making the locomotive more stable and increasing the weight available (some 3 cwt 3 qr) for adhesion on the driving wheels. *Novelty*'s weight was not quite evenly distributed, weighing 1 ton 13 cwt 2 qrs at the bellows end and 1 ton 14 cwt 1 qr at the boiler end.

Right: *Novelty*'s original left-hand cylinder, incorporated into the 1929 replica. Exhaust steam vented directly to the atmosphere. (Author/MSI Manchester)

Below: *Novelty*'s surprisingly crude valve gear; the gabs had to be manually locked and unlocked from pins on the valve levers. (Author/MSI Manchester)

Detail of one of *Novelty*'s original wheels. (Author/MSI Manchester)

Novelty on Test

Novelty had run successfully, without any load, on 6 October and is reported to have attained a maximum speed of 28 mph. On trial the following day, the blowing mechanism failed. She was to have undergone her first official trial on 9 October but Braithwaite and Ericsson requested more time to get their locomotive ready, and 'the trial ... deferred until the following day'. Thus, *Novelty* underwent her first official test on Saturday 10 October 1829; her fire was lit at just before 10 a.m. (2 hours later than the prescribed time) and steam was raised in 54 minutes. Calculating the 'useful load' *Novelty* was to pull proved difficult compared to *Rocket* or *Sans Pareil* as Nicholas Wood wrote in his notebook:

> Load Assigned to Engine. In Stephenson's Engine, the quantity of Goods & Carriages, or useful weight, inclusive of tender, water and coke was 9-10-3-26. Say 191cwt. The weight of the Engine 85cwt. The ratio being 85:191. Then as 85:191::61 (weight of Braithwaite and Ericsson's Engine): 137 the weight to be taken exclusive of water and fuel.
>
> The above measurement taken of Braithwaite's engine taking the Fuel and Water upon the Engine and not in a Tender separate from it as with Stephenson's. We therefore assigned the same proportion of Goods to Braithwaite's Engine in proportion to its weight, exclusive of water. Tank and Fuel, as we did to Stephenson's exclusion of water cask, tender, & fuel – which as above is 137cwt.
>
> Engine weigh when tank filled with water & 2.0.24 of Coke .. .. .. 3-17-0-14 [NRO. 602/15)

With a load of 5 tons 16 cwt, she commenced her first run, going east at 11:00.28, taking 5 minutes 36 seconds to cover the mile and a half mile course, taking slightly longer (6 minutes 40 seconds) travelling west. Only 12 minutes into the trial *Novelty* was withdrawn with a burst water feed pipe 'in consequence of the Engine Man having shut the cock between the forcing Pump and the Boiler' and 'No further Experiment could be made with the Engine this Day, as to completing the Task'.

The *Manchester Mercury* (13 October 1829) described the incident as 'the accidental explosion of a small copper tube' in the boiler. The pro-*Novelty Mechanics' Magazine* glossed over this run as being merely 'by way of rehearsal' rather than being an official part of the competition, and the burst pipe a minor mishap. It is likely that the water pump had been damaged in his mishap, but the damage had not been recognised, as it would fail four days later. The broken pipe was 'sent to Prescott, a distance of two miles', which the *Mechanics' Magazine* thought showed sloppy planning on behalf of the Liverpool & Manchester Railway, because (despite one being on site) 'a forge … with all the necessary tools and materials' was not immediately at hand. While *Novelty* was out of action, *Rocket* was 'exercised' to entertain the crowd and, when uncoupled from her tender, reached a top speed of 30 mph – highly dangerous, and 'as it carried with it neither fuel nor water, it was not a speed which it could have long sustained'.

The 1979 replica in steam, with an appropriately attired crew, at Liverpool Road Station, Manchester, in 2005. (David Boydell)

In order to see fair play, the three judges gave Braithwaite and Ericsson a week's grace to repair *Novelty*, but Braithwaite forced their hand in bringing forward the trial:

> Messrs. Braithwaite & Erickson's Engine appeared to us not likely to be ready before Monday & it was agreed with a Friend of Mr. Braithwaite's (he not being present himself) that they should enter upon the trial of their Engine on Monday morning.
>
> On Friday morning, however, Mr Braithwaite waited upon us at Liverpool in company with his friend and declared that his engine would be all complete and ready for entering upon the task on Saturday morning, and insisted that his Engine should be put on trial on that Day, although we did every thing in our power to induce him to defer the trial until the Monday, being well aware that several joints were to be made which it would be almost impossible to get done in time to allow of their setting.

A surprised John Rastrick wrote in his notebook:

> 14 Oct. 1829 (Wednesday). Messrs. Braithwaite and Ericsson's Engine, having the boiler all in Pieces, when we arrived this morning, and as all the joints were to be made, which took till 0H-23M-15S [12.23pm] before the Boiler could be filled & the fire [illegible]. The steam was up at 1H-15M-15S, which made the time getting up the steam 0-52-0. The fuel being used getting up the steam was about 26 Pounds of Coke. [NRM 1945-108]

Novelty was wheeled to the starting post, and started her first run (according to Rastrick) at 13:25.40. Her first run heading east was 11 minutes 8 seconds; her return trip was much faster, taking a mere 5 minutes 35 seconds. Slowing, reversing and heading east, her second trip was slightly slower, 6 minutes 14 seconds, but after slowing and reversing to head back west, at 14:01.45 'A boiler joint blew out. Stopped the Engine just about the Bridge', and the trial was halted. Following this third major failure, Rastrick recorded: 'In about half an hour after, Mr Ericsson came up to me and stated he had withdrawn his Engine as to any further Contest for the 500 Pounds.' (NRM 1945-108)

The *Mechanics' Magazine* wrote:

> One or two other parts of the machinery that were in a faulty state, had also been renovated; but the engine, with the exception of some of the flanges of the boiler being as Mr Ericsson expressed it, rather *green*, was pronounced in a working state ... just at is completed its second trip of three miles ... the new cement of some of the flanges of the boiler, yielded to the high temperature to which it was exposed. [*Mechanics' Magazine*, 17 October 1829]

The water level in the boiler had dropped too low, uncovering the copper flue tube, which over-heated and collapsed. Clearly, the water pump had been damaged during the mishap with it a few days earlier. The *Manchester Mercury* (20 October 1829) squarely put the blame on Braithwaite and Ericsson for the failure of *Novelty*:

> In consequence of the number of petty accidents which has occurred to the London engine, the "Novelty", the ingenious inventors, Messrs. Braithwaite and Ericsson (rather

unadvisedly as we consider it) took their engine to pieces after the performance of Saturday, and they only had the joints of the boiler pipe closed *this morning*. Every engineer knows the effect of high pressure upon a green joint, but as the "Novelty" had been entered for this day's contest, the proprietors determined upon starting. Accordingly, at one o'clock the engine set off, and performed about seven miles ... when the joint of the boiler pipe gave way, as might have naturally been expected, and the engine was obliged to stop ... It will evidently require several weeks to perfect the working order of the machine.

Rather than Braithwaite having rushed *Novelty*'s repairs, the *Mechanics' Magazine* deflected blame from him; the 'yielding of the cement' (which was still wet) on the joints had been caused through poorly laid track, and was not any fault of the builders of *Novelty*.

Many did not accept the *Mechanics' Magazine*'s version of events: one French commentator noted that the boiler flue had collapsed while the man from *The Times* thought 'the pressure of the steam was too great for the boiler, which burst'. One eye-witness wrote that:

The flue-pipe, passing through the boiler, burst, and of course the working of the engine was suspended. The cause of this accident has been erroneously stated by the *Mechanics' Magazine* to have been the giving way of a *green* cement joint, whereas it was a virtual

The replica certainly confirms John Dixon's observation that *Novelty* had a 'parlour-like appearance', all polished copper and brass like a new tea-kettle. (David Boydell)

bursting of the boiler, the pipe which burst being an essential part of the construction of the engine, which opened a connection between the interior of the boiler and the external air. [*Chester Chronicle*, 13 November 1829]

In reply to the many critics who claimed that the boiler had burst, John Braithwaite fumed in a letter to the *Mechanics' Magazine* that:

There was no giving way of the boiler at all ... but a yielding of part of the furnace-flue, in consequence of its being accidentally exposed to a dry heat of high temperature. [*Mechanics' Magazine*, 7 November 1829]

He thus denied the claim of the *Mechanics' Magazine* that a joint between the two elements of the boiler had failed, but skirts around the fact that there must have been a problem with the water pump: the flue collapsed from over-heating, which can only have been caused through lack of water. The failure of the cement on the joint between the vertical and horizontal sections of the boiler was due to Braithwaite himself insisting that the trial of *Novelty* took place before the cement had fully cured, and because the water pump had failed. Ericsson reported to the judges that the damaged boiler would require 'at least eight working days' to repair and therefore had to 'honourably' withdraw.

The anti-Stephenson *Liverpool Mercury* concluded its account of the Trials with a piece of florid rhetoric:

The GRAND PRIZE OF PUBLIC OPINION is the one which has been gained by Messrs. Braithwaite and Ericsson, for the Decided Improvement in Safety, simplicity, and the smoothness and steadiness of a locomotive engine ... It is beyond doubt, and we believe we speak the opinion of nine-tenths of the engineers and scientific men now in Liverpool, that it is the principle and arrangement of the London engine which must be followed in the construction of all future locomotives. [*Liverpool Mercury*, 16 October 1829]

CHAPTER 3

Unparalleled[3]

We have already met Timothy Hackworth in Chapter 1. Hackworth was an experienced engineer, having previously worked at Wylam Colliery under Christopher Blackett (1751–1829) (the owner) and William Hedley (1779–1843) (the 'Viewer' or colliery manager), and he was probably involved with the design and construction of *Puffing Billy* and *Wylam Dilly* in 1813. Indeed, these two locomotives share several features with the later engines of Hackworth, most notably a Trevithick-inspired U-shaped return flue boiler with the fire grate and chimney at the same end, meaning the driver and fireman were placed at either end of the locomotive. He thus had experience of building and, from 1825 onwards, maintaining locomotives. He would have been very familiar with the Stephenson & Co. locomotives supplied to the Stockton & Darlington, which he maintained at Soho Works, New Shildon. Unfortunately for both concerns, with Robert Stephenson in South America (1824–28), George was both trying to manage at Forth Street and survey the Liverpool & Manchester Railway. George Stephenson and Hackworth, from their correspondence, appear to have been on good terms, George frequently asking Timothy what he thought of the new locomotives he was sending to him for use on the Stockton & Darlington.

Hackworth was a devout Methodist, and was a lay preacher too. As a result, like his rivals the Stephensons, he would have found himself discriminated against by the law because he was not an Anglican, and considered 'beyond the pale' by many of his contemporaries. Methodism, originally a movement within the Church of England led by the Revd John Wesley (1703–91), attracted many converts, especially among the working class; Methodism also inspired self-sufficiency and self-improvement. Hackworth probably left Wylam Colliery, and the village of his birth, because of his Methodist activities (preaching, handing out Bibles and tracts), and refusing to work on Sundays (the Stephensons had no such qualms). Hackworth's wife, Ann, had even been thrown out of her parental home by her strict Anglican parents when she became a Methodist. Timothy named his eldest son, John Wesley Hackworth (1820–91), in

---

3 'Sans pareil' also translates as unexampled, unmatched, unequalled, or peerless.

Left: The original *Sans Pareil* as preserved at Locomotion, the NRM out-station at Shildon, a stone's throw from where she was built in 1829. (Lauren Jaye Gradwell)

Below: A preserved fragment of Hackworth's 'Soho Works' at Shildon.

Hackworth's beautifully restored home, Soho House, at Shildon.

honour of the founder of his faith. Hackworth and George Stephenson were similar in many ways: born in the same pit village; skilled, intuitive mechanics; with little in the way of formal education, and considered outsiders because of their religious belief and practice.

Royal George and *Victory*

Because no one had ever run steam locomotives over such long distances as the Stockton & Darlington Railway, the four locomotives (*Active, Hope, Black Diamond, Diligence*) supplied by the Forth Street Works were often found incapable of sustaining steam pressure for their entire run. Thus, the lacklustre performance of the Stephenson locomotives resulted in Hackworth seeking permission from the Quaker proprietors of the Stockton & Darlington to build his own locomotive: the *Royal George*.

Hackworth used parts from an earlier machine, nicknamed the 'Chittaprat' from the unusual noise it made. 'Chittaprat' was perhaps the first four-cylinder locomotive and had the cranks set at 90 degrees from each other. *Royal George* was to have six coupled driving wheels of Hackworth's own pattern. The two cylinders were mounted at the rear end of the boiler, working downwards directly on the crank pin of the trailing wheel set. The piston rod was guided not by slide bars, but by parallel motion. The boiler – the shell of which

39

Hackworth's *Royal George* of 1828, considered to be the most advanced and powerful locomotive of its day.

came from 'Chittaprat' – was fitted with a return-flue boiler in the manner of Trevithick so that the chimney and firebox were at the same end. To prevent enginemen from holding down their lever safety valves, Hackworth invented a sprung safety valve, using a stack of leaf springs to hold down the valve. *Royal George* first ran on 29 November 1827 and was an instant success, being a better steamer and having more power than the four Stephenson locomotives. *Royal George* partially solved the Stockton & Darlington's motive power crisis, and furthermore showed the supremacy of the locomotive over horses. It is no surprise that Hackworth's second locomotive, completed in 1829, was named *Victory*.

Sans Pareil

Hackworth's Rainhill entry, *Sans Pareil*, was based on lessons learnt from maintaining the early products of the Forth Street Works as well as his two previous locomotives. In order to meet the strict weight stipulations, *Sans Pareil* was an 0-4-0 rather than a heavy-weight 0-6-0. In contrast to *Rocket*, which was built at Forth Street Works by a well-financed full-time team, *Sans Pareil* was built alongside Hackworth's day job of keeping the locomotives and stationary engines of the Stockton & Darlington Railway in running order, with the capital to build her coming from his own pocket. Many of her key components were out-sourced, including the boiler and cylinders.

Sans Pareil's boiler, measuring 6 feet (1.8 m) long and 4 feet 2 inches (1.2 m) diameter, was made at the Bedlington Foundry, from eight wrought-iron plates lap-riveted together. The flat front end of the boiler is built up from several flat plates, while the convex rear end is made from eight plates around the perimeter with a single large plate in the centre. Running through the boiler was a wrought-iron U-shaped return flue, tapering from a diameter of 2 feet (60 cm) at the grate end to 19 inches (48 cm) at the apex of the 'U' and 15 inches (38 cm) at the chimney. This tapered flue tube was designed to increase the flow of hot gasses

Above: *Sans Pareil* as depicted by the *Mechanics' Magazine*; it was essentially a scaled-down version of *Royal George*. Note that the illustrator has incorrectly placed the tender at the opposite end of the locomotive to the firebox (which was at the chimney end).

Right: *Sans Pareil*'s boiler: firegrate (A), U-shaped conical flue tube (B), chimney (C), water jacket (D). (Andrew Mason after John Rastrick)

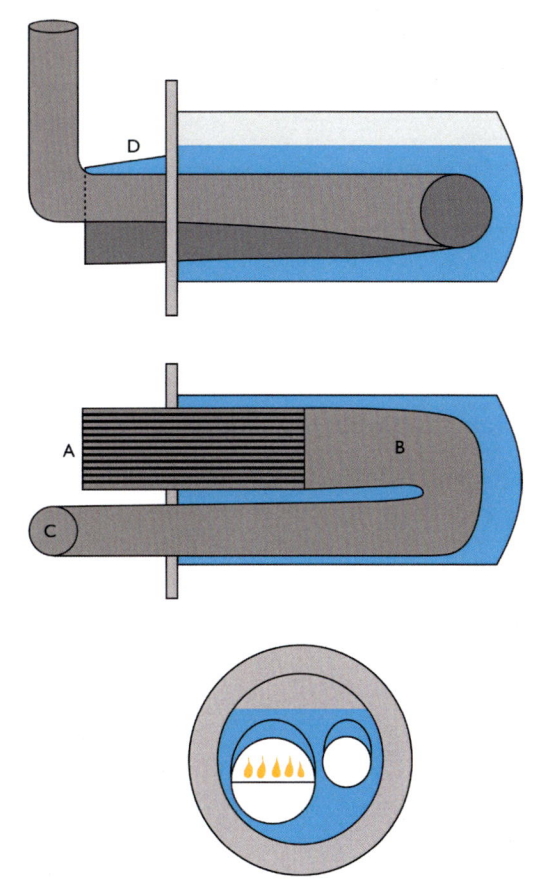

through the fire and boiler, improving the heating characteristics. To increase the amount of surface area in direct contact and heated by the fire, Hackworth provided a 2-foot (60 cm) long extension to his flue tube, which was covered on its upper surface by a half-round water jacket. Rastrick shows this water jacket having a maximum depth of 6 inches (15.2 cm), together with an accompanying water jacket at the chimney end of the main flue. The firebars were 5 feet (1.52 m) long, giving a grate area of 10 square feet. It would have been a difficult job for the fireman to shovel coke from the swaying tender, over the gap between the two vehicles and into the furnace; he also had to regularly clear out the ashes which fell through the fire bars so as not to impede flow of primary air through the fire.

The Stephensons were well aware of *Sans Pareil*'s boiler design, Robert considering at the start of August 1829 that, 'He [Hackworth] does not appear to understand that a coke fire will only burn briskly where the escape of the carbonic acid gas [carbon dioxide] is immediate.' In other words, Robert thought that the draughting arrangements of *Sans Pareil*'s boiler were poor, with a slow throughput of gasses. Robert further wrote that:

> He has a double tube as usual, but he makes the boiler only 5 ft. [sic, 6] long. Beyond the length he supplies the deficiency in length by a small cylinder around the fire tube which he makes surround it ½ inch from it; this clearly saves weight, but I think not to the extent he anticipated, for his boiler ... including tubes, weighs 2 tons 3 or 4 cwts. He saves in water; decidedly on this point we are about equal ... The part of the tube which projects beyond the boiler, and which contains the fire is not continued below the firebars, so that the part which projects is only a semi-cylinder. [RAIL 1008/88/1/3]

He continued on 26 August, opining that:

> The projecting part of Hackworth's tube will be very liable to burn away from the water being blown into the large part of the boiler. We must, however, leave him alone. [RAIL 1008/88/1/4]

Rastrick also shows a similar water jacket over the base of the chimney, probably trying to extract the maximum amount of heat from the boiler gases. Unlike *Rocket*, there were no circulating pipes from the boiler to the water jacket to encourage water flow around the hottest part of the fire. John Wesley Hackworth complained in later life that the boiler was of 'a most imperfect workmanship' and leaked badly.

Sans Pareil's cylinders were mounted vertically at the rear of the locomotive, driving downwards acting on spherical crank pins on the trailing wheels. The piston rod was guided by square-section slide bars, supporting a crosshead slipper – an improvement on the earlier arrangement used on *Victory*, which used cylindrical slide bars. The cylinders had a bore of 7 inches and a stroke of 18. They were cast by the Stephensons at Forth Street, and of them J. W. Hackworth, remembering events of twenty-eight years earlier (he was only nine years old at the time of the Rainhill Trials), complained:

> The cylinders were made at Messrs. Stephenson's, and were very indifferently manufactured; one of them burst at the commencement of the trial; the fault was in the

thickness of the metal forming the partition between the bore of the cylinder, and the port-way or steam pipe, along the side of the cylinder, which had been cast and bored so thin in one part as to leave less than 1-16ths of an inch of metal. [I saw] a piece of metal that was broken off round the edge of the fracturing which was about the thickness of an old sixpence ... the burst in the cylinder was not external – such as all the world could have seen and understood. [*The Engineer*, 14 August 1857]

Thus, when the slide valve on the damaged cylinder opened, 'An unusually powerful steam jet [at full boiler pressure] issuing from the blast pipe caused a great quantity of fuel to be ejected from the fire grate.'

While supporters of Hackworth have claimed that this fault may have been deliberate sabotage, it has to be remembered that the Stephensons cast six cylinders for Hackworth, due to the unreliability of using floating cores to produce cylinders cast with integral steam chests. Indeed, when cylinders for the replica *Rocket* were made in 1979, eight castings had to be made because of the problem with obtaining a perfect casting due to the cylinder design. The design was quickly changed for the next batch of Stephenson locomotives, obviating this difficulty. It was probably just bad luck that lead to *Sans Pareil* having one 'imperfect' cylinder, the fault in which could not be readily examined.

Sans Pareil's valve gear followed that of *Victory*: a pair of loose, limited-travel eccentrics, fitted over a sleeve that was keyed and clamped to the driving axle. The eccentrics were maintained in correct alignment via flanges towards each end of the sleeve. Driving dogs, set at 90º to each other, fitted to the sleeve drove the eccentrics; curved (semi-circular) slots in the eccentrics allowed them to slip until they found the correct position for forward or reverse gear. The eccentric rods, as on *Victory*, were curved to pass around the hemispherical end of the boiler. They terminated with gab-hooks, which engaged with pins on the valve handles that in turn drove the horizontal rocking shaft, which worked the valve spindles. This system was clearly efficient as *Sans Pareil* had a quicker 'turn round' time at the end of each run than *Rocket*.

Two controversies surround *Sans Pareil*: whether or not she had springs, and the form – and indeed progenitor – of the blast pipe. The remains of *Sans Pareil* lack any form of frame, with the axle boxes being riveted directly to the boiler barrel, a feature shared by the 1979 replica. *Royal George* and *Victory* certainly had frames; therefore it is likely that *Sans Pareil* as built had a frame. For *Sans Pareil* to have not been so built would certainly be a retrograde step – even if it was omitted to save weight – and would certainly preclude the fitting of springs as stipulated in the Trial Conditions. It is likely that the lack of a frame is due to the restoration of *Sans Pareil* by John Hick in 1864: although the original boiler brackets to which the frame would have been attached survive, additional vertical brackets were added during this 'restoration' to carry the axle boxes. Because of the downward thrust of the vertical cylinders, *Royal George* lacked springs on its driving wheels, but the leading wheel sets were sprung. *Rocket*'s driving wheels, because of the use of inclined cylinders, however, could be sprung. The likelihood, therefore, is that *Sans Pareil* had springs, whose arrangement probably followed that of *Royal George* or *Victory*, with the leading wheels being sprung and the driving wheels unsprung. If the driving wheels were sprung, then Hackworth would have had to increase the 'swept area' of his cylinders, to account for the additional vertical movement of the piston caused by the springs. Alan Middleton, who drove the replica *Sans Pareil* when it was running in Manchester, says that the locomotive has a pronounced yaw from side to side on each stroke of the piston, leading to the driver having a sense of sea-sickness at anything above walking pace. George Stephenson's assistant John Dixon wrote in a letter to his brother James on 16 October 1829:

> He ... mumbles and roars and rolls about like a Empty Beer Butt on a rough Pavement ... and as for being on Springs I must confess I cannot find them out either going or standing, neither can I perceive any effect they have. [Warren: 206]

It is likely that because of *Sans Pareil*'s very short wheelbase and vertical cylinders, the springing of the leading wheels was ineffective. If, however, both axles were sprung, then the thrust of the pistons would be partially absorbed by the springs, and would certainly account for her rolling around 'like an Empty Beer Butt.' Indeed, *Rocket*, at speed, has a wobble because of the thrust of her – albeit diagonal – pistons on a sprung axle. The lowering of the cylinders on the locomotives that came after *Rocket* to 8º would have largely negated this problem. It seems unlikely for such a competent engineer as Timothy

Sans Pareil raising steam in Manchester, 2005, clearly in breach of the stipulation that 'Engines must consume their own smoke'! (David Boydell)

Hackworth, whose reputation and his personal capital were tied up in *Sans Pareil*, to neglect to fit springs, and thus be automatically disqualified from the Rainhill Trials.

The second controversy is the blast pipe, and the form it took on *Sans Pareil*. The *Mechanics' Magazine* (31 October 1829) noted that:

> The 'Sans Pareil' of Mr Ackworth is of the same principle as the 'Rocket'; the combustion of the fuel being effected by the *exhausting power of the chimney*, and the ejection of steam from the cylinders into the chimney.

In other words, both locomotives used exhaust steam to liven up their fire, an effect first noted by Richard Trevithick more than twenty years earlier. Unlike *Rocket*, *Sans Pareil* had a single exhaust or 'eduction pipe', exactly the same as *Puffing Billy* or *Wylam Dilly* from over a decade before. On *Rocket* the open ends of the eduction pipes were turned up into the chimney, à la Trevithick, but on *Sans Pareil*, copying the *Royal George*, the eduction pipe was fitted with a rather phallic coned nozzle, which increased the pressure and therefore speed of the exhaust steam ejected by the blast pipe. Despite a lengthy, and often acrimonious, correspondence in the pages of *The Engineer* during 1857, Robert Stephenson admitted that the use of a coned blast pipe nozzle was due to Hackworth on the *Royal George*. He wrote:

> The single steam-blast having been in existence eleven years prior to the opening of the Stockton and Darlington Railway ... it had actually been in regular use since the year 1814, and the only alteration which it underwent, was the contraction of the orifice made on the Stockton and Darlington Railway ... between ... 1825 and 1827 ... I believe to be due to Timothy Hackworth. [S. Smiles: 503]

Robert Stephenson blamed the propensity of *Sans Pareil* to throw fire on the blast pipe orifice being too restricted. That said, the replica of *Sans Pareil* does not share the same propensity, and as J. W. Hackworth believed, it was probably due to the cracked cylinder, with steam from the boiler bypassing the piston at full boiler pressure and being ejected through the blast pipe, which led to the 'fire throwing'.

Sans Pareil on Trial

Unlike *Rocket* or *Novelty*, which were transported to Liverpool by water, *Sans Pareil* was transported to Crown Street yard by road. The *Mechanics' Magazine* described *Sans Pareil* as:

> In ... general appearance, particularly in its large dimensions, a near resemblance to Mr. Stephenson's engine; but it is much more compactly arranged, and on account of this ... travels with much greater steadiness ... The furnace and boiler are of simple construction, and of unquestionable efficiency; but their great size, and the large supply of water and fuel they require, render them ... ill-adapted to ... a locomotive engine. [*Mechanics' Magazine*, 31 October 1829]

The *Annales des Ponts et Chaussées* was of a similar opinion:

> The Sans-Pareil of Mr Hackworth. The construction of this machine is very much similar as the machines in usage on the [Stockton and] Darlington Railway. The fire is contained in a tube, which is extended in the interior of the boiler, and which returns near about its point of origin. The same as in the Novelty, the cylinders are vertical, and the pistons work ... using triangular cranks which are externally connected to the two wheels of the leading end. [*Annales des Ponts et Chaussées* (1831): 10]

Unfortunately for Hackworth, because *Sans Pareil* had had no running-in trials, several faults reared their heads. The *Annales des Ponts et Chaussées* reported that 'through some defect' with her boiler, *Sans Pareil* was 'not subject of an experiment' on the first day of the trials (6 October); and on the following day 'the Judges accorded to Mr Hackworth the time necessary to remedy' the leaks in the boiler. J. W. Hackworth describes the joints in the boiler as being so bad that copper had 'to be run and caulked to make them steam tight' and it took Hackworth until late on Monday 12 October to get *Sans Pareil* in working order. John Dixon wrote that:

> Timothy has been sadly out of temper ever since he came here for he has been grobbing on day and night and nothing our men did for him was right. He was most unhappy with

With safety-valve blowing, *Sans Pareil* charges across Water Street Bridge, Manchester. (David Boydell)

the tender. He openly accused George Stephenson's people from conspiring to hinder him, of which I do believe them innocent. [Warren: 206]

Sans Pareil was in steam and tested overnight to check 'if some leaks in the boiler ... had been effectually stopped' and thus at 8 a.m. on the damp and cold morning of Tuesday 13 October, she was still in steam. This meant that the judges could not measure the amount of coke necessary for her to raise steam, 'but', thought the *Annales des Ponts et Chaussées*, 'this matter is of little importance.' With her safety valve spitting, *Sans Pareil* was wheeled onto the weighing machine and found (in working order) to be 4 tons 15 cwt 2 qrs, or more than 600 lbs over the weight limit for a four-wheeled locomotive. *The Times*, however, reported *Sans Pareil* weighed only 4 tons 8 cwt 2 qrs, and was therefore under the stipulated weight limit for a four-wheeled locomotive. *Sans Pareil* should have been disqualified, but according to Nicholas Wood, the three judges 'determined to put the engine through the same trial, as if it conformed to the proposed conditions' to 'ascertain if the performance was such as would enable them to recommend this point to the favourable consideration of the Directors'. Because *Sans Pareil* had such a short wheelbase, 'All the wheels of the Engine stood upon the plate of the Weighing Machine' and 'was ... all weighed at once.' *Rocket*, due to her longer wheelbase, had had to be weighed twice: first the driving wheels, then the carrying wheels. The tender – built by the Worsdells at Crown Street – carried 300 gallons of water (weighing 1 ton 6 cwt 3 qrs 4 lbs) and 6 cwt of coke. Total weight of the tender was 3 tons 6 cwt 3 qrs. The total load assigned to *Sans Pareil* was therefore 14 tons 6 cwt 2 qr.

Rastrick recorded:

Having been at work all night, when we arrived the water in the Boiler was quite hot. It was therefore useless to attempt to ascertain the quantity of coke it had used in bringing up the steam, or the time required for that purpose at this time. We proposed to do this at another Opportunity. [NRM 1945-108]

Sans Pareil moved off from the starting post at 10:10.21, running the eastward lap of the measured one and a half miles in 5 minutes 9 seconds; the return trip was more than 2 minutes slower, at 7 minutes 37 seconds. Fifty minutes into the experiment, after having completed seven full runs (out and back) and returning from the first leg of her eighth run, *Sans Pareil*'s fusible plug burned out.

The fusible plug is an early warning device. It is made from bronze and has a lead core, and is screwed into to the crown of the firebox. If the crown becomes overheated because the water level is too low, the lead core will melt out and a jet of steam will issue into the firebox with a loud hissing noise, alerting the crew. To ascertain the water level, *Sans Pareil* was fitted with three try-cocks, which straddled the working water level of the boiler; when opened, the top cock should issue steam; the centre (on the waterline) steam and water; and the bottom just water. But, because the boiling water in the boiler would instantly flash to steam, it could be a tricky job to accurately gauge how much water was in the boiler. *Rocket*, conversely, had two try-cocks at the front of the boiler where they could not be easily accessed. Instead, she used the revolutionary technology of a gauge glass – a thick glass tube connected to the boiler by two cocks, straddling the water level – which at a glance would show the water level in the boiler.

48

Right: Fireman's view of *Sans Pareil*: unlike the original, the replica has a modern gauge glass and pressure gauge to assist in the safe working of the boiler. (David Boydell)

Opposite above: The fireman attends to *Sans Pareil*'s fire, which needed regular attention to keep it free from ash and clinker. He had the precarious job of shovelling coal into the firebox over the gap between the tender and boiler. (David Boydell)

Opposite below: Chalked instructions for filling *Sans Pareil*'s water barrel! (David Boydell)

The water level in *Sans Pareil*'s boiler had dropped so low, uncovering the crown of the fire tube, because the water feed pump (driven off her right-hand cylinder cross-head) was not working. Rastrick noted *Sans Pareil* had made seven and a half trips in 1 hour 37 minutes, equating to 22½ miles, and had consumed all but 8 inches of water in her tender tank. Nicholas Wood wrote in his notes:

> [The Engine] At 0.55 [12.55] came to the watering place near the Smith's Shop being brought up by men from the Grand Stand in consequence of the Pump getting out of order, checking the supply of water to the Boiler, which getting below the top of the Tube the Lead Plug melted out. [NRO 620/15]

Wood also notes that the crew of *Sans Pareil* had been trying to get water into the boiler at the end of the sixth and seventh runs; they spent over four minutes 'Greasing and repairing [the] Pump' and were able to 'take in 16 imperial gallons' of water during the seventh trip.

After the locomotive had cooled sufficiently to allow the work to take place, a second fusible plug was screwed in to the fire tube crown. Rastrick commented in his notebook:

> The plug was put in again and the fire lighted and the cask was well filled at 1.30 and the Steam was got up again at 2.15 but the forcing Pump, having gone wrong again, the further prosecution of the Experiment was abandoned. [NRM 1945-108]

The man from *The Times* reported how:

> For two hours, this engine [*Sans Pareil*] performed with great speed and regularity, averaging full 14 miles an hour, for a distance of upwards of 25 miles, while drawing that enormous load. Unfortunately, one of the pumps which supply the boiler with water from the tender was out of order, and, in consequence, some accident occurred, which it was necessary to stop to remedy. [*The Times*, 16 October 1829]

The *Manchester Mercury* considered that:

> This is no proof of failure, because it has nothing to do with the principle: and we are assured that when the "Sanspareil" has got into good working order, she will rank high on the list of competitors, and may well be even considered as having fulfilled the original conditions. [*Manchester Mercury*, 20 October 1829]

One of the observers of *Sans Pareil* had a lucky escape: 'On one occasion, a man fell, by some accident, within the rails,' as Sans Pareil was 'approaching with great rapidity'. Luckily, 'having had the presence of mind to lay down, the machine passed over him without doing him any injury.' While *Sans Pareil* was out of action, Hackworth had the frustration of seeing *Rocket* 'exercising ... which, without carrying any weight, performed several journies at a speed exceeding its former performances' much to the 'delight' of the crowd.

Hackworth immediately 'demanded that he be accorded with a new experiment for *Sans Pareil*'. The three judges, however,

> Refused him, on the basis that not only had the machine exceeded the stipulated weight limit, but also that the mode of construction did not seem to them a sufficient value of recommendation to the directors of the company. [*Annales des Ponts et Chaussées* (1831): 14]

Nicholas Wood's analysis of *Sans Pareil* shows that she attained a maximum speed of $22^{2}/_{3}$ miles per hour, having burned 1,269 lbs of coke and evaporated 274 imperial gallons of water. Something was clearly wrong with the locomotive: the high fuel consumption was perhaps due to the over-zealous coning of the blast pipe nozzle, and the high water consumption from the apparently leaking cylinder. Hackworth is reputed to have blamed the Stephensons and Michael Longridge at Bedlington Ironworks for their poor workmanship. His son, John Wesley, not content to cast aspersions at Stephenson or Longridge, believed that there had been what amounted to industrial sabotage at Rainhill itself, with Messrs Stephenson sending a spy, under the cover of darkness, to study and copy *Sans Pareil*'s blast pipe. The idea was quickly refuted, but clearly shows the bitterness of the Hackworth camp toward their former friends and allies.

The leaks in the boiler could have been due to poorly aligned plates; rivets not being hot enough when closed over; the plates being of uneven thickness; or from damage in transit. That said, Hackworth probably chose the Bedlington Ironworks because they had a reputation for the quality of iron plates they produced and their experience making locomotive boilers. While a badly cast or bored cylinder would have been difficult to

Sans Pareil and her coach clatter past Liverpool Road Station and over Water Street Bridge. The driver's position was somewhat precarious. (David Boydell)

identify, the boiler was presumably hydraulically tested to three times its working pressure at Bedlington, as per the Rainhill Trial stipulations. A modern boilersmith has suggested that such excessive testing could easily have been the cause of the leaks.

After completion *Sans Pareil* was run just once on the Aycliffe level (on the Stockton & Darlington) at midnight before being dispatched to Liverpool. A steam leak would not have been noticeable if the boiler had been lagged, hiding the evidence for any defect. After arriving at Crown Street she would presumably have been steam tested. But, as J. W. Hackworth asserts, there was not enough time and *Sans Pareil* was only steam tested at Rainhill, where it was found that the boiler was leaking badly enough to be obvious through the boiler cladding. The feed pump was also found to be faulty or damaged. A minor leak, perhaps the result of the hydraulic test, which had been hidden before she left for Liverpool could have been aggravated by rough handling on the road, resulting in a major leak which meant that steam and water were visibly issuing from the boiler.

To caulk up these leaks, the timber cladding and layers of felt had to be removed, the boiler brought up to working pressure, the leaks identified and then cooled so that copper could be caulked into the leaky joint. J. W. Hackworth suggests that his father used two processes to seal the leaks on his boiler: firstly, pouring molten copper into the joint, and, once it had cooled, caulking it into the joint. John Dixon thought that Hackworth stopped up the leaking boiler using the traditional method of oatmeal added to the boiler water, 'more ... than would fatten a pig'. The use of molten copper run into the joint was not be guaranteed to work, and by effectively being cast copper the final result would be very brittle and liable to fracture when being hammered into the joint. A modern boilersmith recommends the use of an annealed copper strip, which is caulked into the joint, as the use of molten copper would 'not have served any proper purpose'.

Unfortunately, this process could also lead to the leaks becoming worse due to stress from a rapid heating–cooling cycle and from the hammer blows from the caulking process itself: Robert Wilson, an Inspector for the earliest national (albeit voluntary) boiler inspectorate, the Manchester Steam Users Association, thought that 'the jarring caused by the caulking is no doubt liable to start the seams, and cause fresh leakage' under pressure. He concluded that caulking a leaking boiler, especially under steam, was a dangerous process, and that the leak 'is usually aggravated by caulking and hammering all the time at

Rivals re-united: replicas of *Rocket* and *Sans Pareil* running side-by-side over Water Street Bridge in 2005. (David Boydell)

leaky rivets and joints, the principle is inherently bad ...' Hackworth's attempt at sealing a small leak by hammering and caulking might in fact have made the problem much worse!

It is also likely that with so much time devoted to the boiler, Hackworth and his men overlooked the faulty feed pump – or were unaware the pump was faulty – in the rush to repair the boiler. Of the cracked cylinder, Timothy Hackworth, writing to the judges immediately after Rainhill, states that one of them did indeed leak: 'The defects were of nature easily to be remedied ... the whole alteration which has been made is the removal of a cylinder, which failed from its defective casting.' [NRM HACK 1-1-25]

Thus, John Wesley Hackworth's contention that the construction of *Sans Pareil* was rushed (in Hackworth's spare time) and, 'as the engine could only be taken to Liverpool by common cart' in a lengthy journey by road, 'the time taking for its transport forbade a practical test' is probably correct. So too is his assertion that there was a faulty cylinder. Though there is no definite evidence of industrial sabotage beyond the fact that the cylinders and boiler were made by the Stephensons or their allies, the failure of *Sans Pareil*, on a mechanical level, was certainly due to circumstances out of the control of Timothy Hackworth and his team. No wonder his later supporters took up such bitter cudgels in his defence, and against the perceived Stephensonian bias of the Liverpool & Manchester directors. On these grounds, Hackworth had every right to demand a second trial, but was denied by Messrs Kennedy, Rastrick and Wood. Whether *Sans Pareil* could have won, on a technological level, will be examined in Chapter 6.

Chapter 4

The *Rocket*

Rocket, like Rainhill itself, is one of the most famous names in railway history and is perhaps one of the few railway locomotives to be recognised by non-enthusiasts, alongside such hallowed names as *Mallard, Flying Scotsman* and *Thomas*. Contrary to popular myths, *Rocket* was not built by George Stephenson and nor was it the 'first' railway locomotive – that distinction goes to the Coalbrookdale locomotive of Richard Trevithick (a friend of the Stephenson family) from 1803.

The earliest known depiction of *Rocket* from the *Mechanics' Magazine*, 24 October 1829. The builders of the 1881, 1929 and 1979 replicas confused one of the safety valves (G) for a steam dome, which *Rocket* lacked at Rainhill.

Rocket was designed and built by the consortium of George and Robert Stephenson and Henry Booth. Although traditionally credited to George alone, it was Robert and Henry Booth who were most involved in the technical design and its implementation. Booth's inventiveness did not end with the boiler for *Rocket*: he designed the sprung buffing- and draw-gear used on the Liverpool & Manchester Railway, as well as a patent axle grease and the three-link screw coupling, a form of which was used into the late twentieth century.

Rocket was built by Robert Stephenson & Co. at their Forth Street Works, Newcastle. The company had been established by George Stephenson for his son, with the help of the wealthy Quaker Edward Pease – his former employer on the Stockton & Darlington – in June 1823. The capital was £4,000 in ten shares, held by Robert Stephenson (two), George Stephenson (two), Pease (four) and Michael Longridge (two). It was the world's first locomotive manufactory. By the time of the Rainhill Trials, the company had constructed about twenty locomotives. The decision to build *Rocket* was initiated by Henry Booth, who recalled:

> I mentioned my scheme to Mr Stephenson, and asked him if he would join me in building a locomotive to compete for the prize of £500 offered by the Directors ... Mr Stephenson took a day or two to look into the merits of the plan I proposed, and then told me he thought it would do, and would join me in the venture. [R. Smiles: 41]

In order to meet the demands of the rules of the Rainhill Trials, *Rocket* was a scaled-down, lighter version of their earlier locomotive *Lancashire Witch*: an 0-2-2 rather than an 0-4-0. Booth had been involved in the design of the boiler of *Lancashire Witch* to enable it to effectively burn coke and therefore 'consume its own smoke' as stipulated by the Liverpool & Manchester Railway Act.

The 2010 replica of *Rocket* standing at the historic Liverpool Road Station during her visit to mark the 180th anniversary of the Liverpool & Manchester Railway. (Matthew Jackson)

Rocket Men

According to the rather sentimental portrait painted by Samuel Smiles, George Stephenson was illiterate until he was eighteen; part of his arrogance and abrasive personality was perhaps to cover up for his lack of formal education. So too his tendency to 'micro-manage' as recorded by Charles Vignoles: 'He does not look on the concern with a liberal and expanded view; but considers it with a microscopic eye and magnifying the importance of details.' Even the Directors of the Liverpool & Manchester thought he had 'a queer temper'.

Henry Booth was a member of a wealthy and influential Unitarian merchant family from Liverpool attending Paradise Street Chapel. Unitarians are free-thinkers who emphasise the use of reason and debate, and reject the imposition of any formal statement of belief, and it was from Unitarians that Robert Stephenson received his education at the Percy Street Academy, Newcastle. Academies such as this had been established by Unitarians because their faith was illegal until 1813, and because they were not only barred an education at parish schools but, until 1854, from the ancient universities of Oxford and Cambridge. Here, Robert came to the attention of the Unitarian Minister Revd William Turner (1761–1859), minister at Hanover Square Unitarian Chapel, Newcastle. Turner was the main founder of the Newcastle Literary and Philosophical Society (1793), of which he was secretary for its first forty-four years. Turner took Robert under his wing and 'was

George Stephenson's cottage at Wylam, Northumberland. (Lauren Jaye Gradwell)

always ready to assist ... with books, with instruments and with council, gratefully and cheerfully. He gave ... the most valuable assistance and instruction.' Thus, Robert, unlike his father, moved in the 'right circles' and with the 'right people.'

After leaving Percy Street, Robert was apprenticed to Nicholas Wood at Killingworth Colliery for three years. After his apprenticeship, he studied at the University of Edinburgh (1822–23) because, unlike their English counterparts, the Scottish universities had no religious test for admission, which meant that someone like Robert, who had studied at a Dissenting Academy, could attend. Robert's inquisitive intellect would have been broadened by his Unitarian education, especially in terms of freedom of thought, engaging with new ideas and 'thinking outside the box.'

Booth's Boilers

Booth's first essay in boiler design was that of the *Lancashire Witch* (1828), which was designed to burn coke, which needs a lot of air to do so efficiently. The earlier single-flue boilers of Stephenson or the return flue of Trevithick, while being suitable for the burning of cheap coal, were not ideally suited to coke. In order to get the coke to burn efficiently, Henry Booth deduced that the number of boiler flues had to be multiplied to increase the throughput of air and combustion products. Booth gained permission to build what would be *Lancashire Witch* from the Liverpool & Manchester Board on 30 April 1827:

> The Treasurer reported that he had discovered a method of producing Steam without Smoke, which he considered might be applied to Locomotive and other Engines; Mr Stephenson attended, and having given his opinion that the Invention, if it succeeded on a large scale, would be highly important to the Company ... was directed to make any experiments necessary. [RAIL371/1]

Booth came up with the idea of using several smaller flue tubes, through which the combustion products would pass. Work began on *Lancashire Witch* in January 1828; George Stephenson noted to Robert, 'You must calculate that this engine will be for all the engineers in the Kingdom – nay, indeed, the world – to look at.' Making the small tubes was quite a complicated job as Booth wrote to Robert Stephenson in April 1828:

> I am quite aware that the bent tubes are a complicated job to make, but after once in and well it cannot be any complication in the working of the engine. The bent tube is a child of your own. [Warren: 141]

It appears there was one main flue, flanked by two of a smaller diameter but uniting in a manifold at the chimney end of the boiler. Running down the centre of the main flue were two oval section water tubes, probably the 'bent tubes' referred to by Booth. Because Stephenson and Booth predicted problems with burning coke without a forced blast of air (think of a blacksmiths' forge), he used a 'pair of bellows worked by eccentrics under the tender', which George had a hand in designing. Henry Booth envisaged the locomotive burning both coal and coke 'better to feed one time with coke and the next with coal.

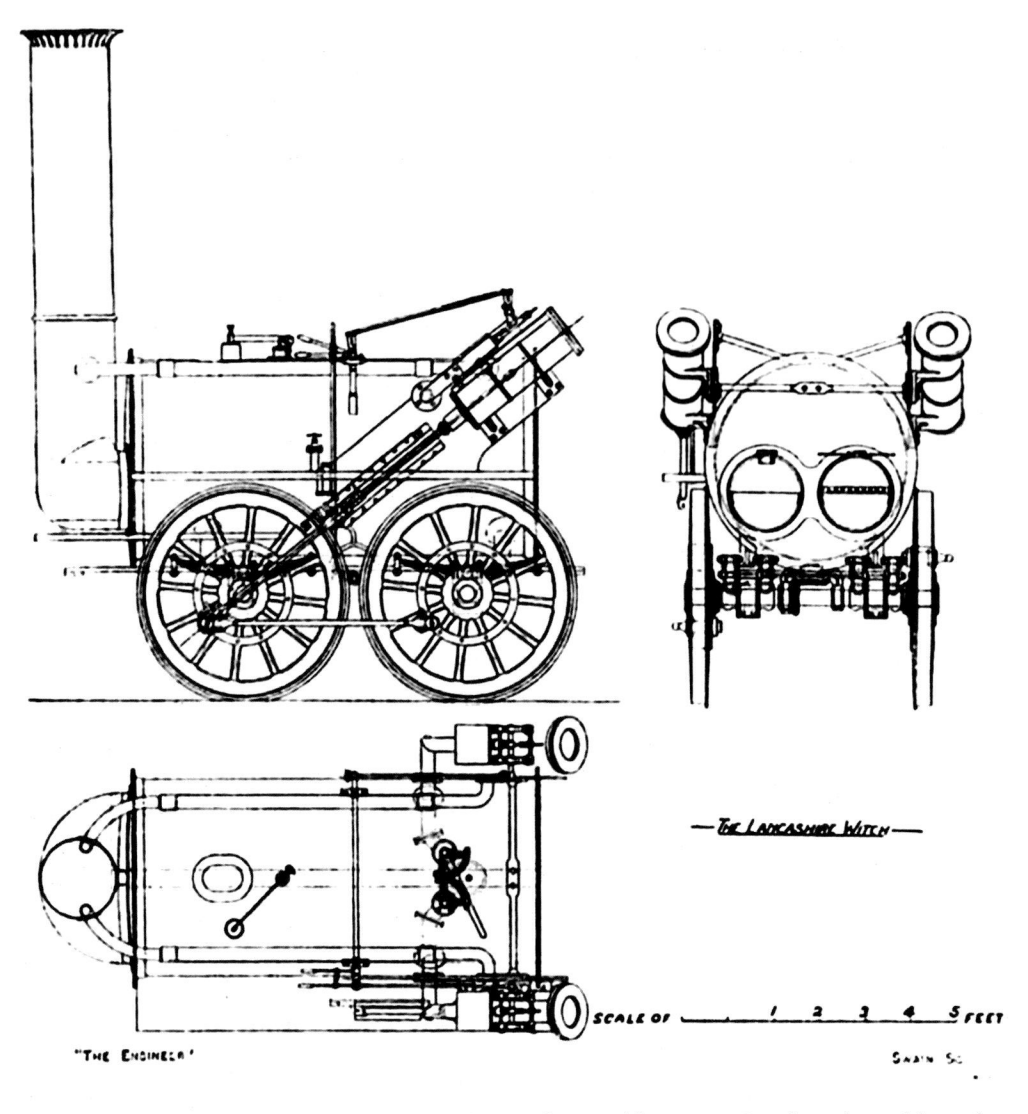

Lancashire Witch (1828), the boiler of which was designed by Henry Booth and was blown by bellows in order to prevent smoke.

I think the one would revive the other'. The engine was finished by July 1828 when George Stephenson wrote to his old colleague, Timothy Hackworth that, '[It] works beautifully. There is not the least noise about it. We have tried the blast [i.e. forced draught from the bellows] for burning coke and I believe it will answer.' [Warren: 142]

The as yet un-named *Lancashire Witch* was delivered to the Bolton & Leigh Railway late in July 1828, and the *London Courier* (Wednesday 13 August 1828) reported that it had hauled a train containing the directors of the Bolton & Leigh, Liverpool & Manchester and 'eminent scientific men' on Friday 1 August, during which ceremony she was named by William Hulton Esq., Chairman of the Bolton & Leigh Railway. Robert Stephenson in his report described how:

It is of eight horse power, and calculated to draw a load of twenty tons, at a rate of seven miles per hour ... In this engine smoke is also partially destroyed, by means of a blast of atmospheric air, which by assisting the combustion of the fuel, so not only increases the intensity of the heat, but allows less to pass off in the shape of smoke. [*London Courier*, 13 August 1828]

In other words, Robert Stephenson, contrary to the suggestion of John Wesley Hackworth in 1857, fully understood the usefulness of an air blast on a coke fire – as witnessed on any coke-fired smithing hearth. He was merely applying existing technology (bellows) to the locomotive, although this would later prove to be a technological dead end because forced-draught locomotives used more energy in working the bellows than in propelling themselves. That this was a dead-end is shown by the fact that the blowing apparatus was subsequently removed from *Lancashire Witch* and it was not used on any later Stephenson locomotive. *Lancashire Witch* was the first Stephenson engine to have diagonal rather than vertical cylinders and direct-drive to the wheels. It also used a variable cut-off 'to economise the fuel ... by working the steam expansively'. As Dr Michael Bailey has described, the Stephenson works between 1828 and 1830 drove rapid technological development of the locomotive, resulting in the delivery of *Planet* – the progenitor of all steam locomotives for the next 130 years – in October 1830.

It is likely that Henry Booth was aware of the concept of the multi-tube boiler, as it had been around for several decades. In France, the Marquis de Jouffroy d'Abbans (1751–1832) – the inventor of the steam boat – had designed a stationary multi-tubular boiler with forty-three fire tubes in 1784, while French chemist and inventor Philippe Gengembre (1764–1838) of the Paris Mint patented a multi-tubular boiler in 1821. Marc Séguin (1786–1875) of Lyons, engineer of the St Etienne Railway, designed a multi-tube boiler in 1825, which he patented in February 1828, and James Neville of London patented his own design of a multi-tube boiler in March 1826. In all these designs, hot gasses passed through tubes surrounded by water, but in his patent application of December 1827 Séguin pre-empted the design of *Rocket* by providing a separate firebox. Séguin's boiler used forty-seven flue tubes – nearly twice as many as *Rocket* – in order to increase the air flow through the boiler, and in order to maintain this flow, Monsieur Pellatan suggested the use of 'a steam-jet in the chimney' analogous to the blast-pipe. Séguin began construction of his two locomotives with multi-tubular boilers in May 1829, mere months before work commenced on *Rocket*. Sadly for Séguin, *Rocket* was completed a month ahead of Séguin's locomotive, and won eternal fame at Rainhill. Late in life, Isaac Watt Boulton noted, 'I have been long convinced that the idea did not originate with Mr Booth. I believe it came from France.' Thus, while the idea of a multi-tubular boiler was clearly not new, applying it successfully to a locomotive was. Booth later wrote that:

This new plan of boiler comprised the introduction of numerous small tubes, two or three inches in diameter, less than an eighth of an inch thick, through which to carry the fire ... we not only obtain[ed] a very much larger heating surface, but the heating surface is much more effective, as there intervenes between the fire and the water only a thin sheet of copper. [R. Smiles: 41]

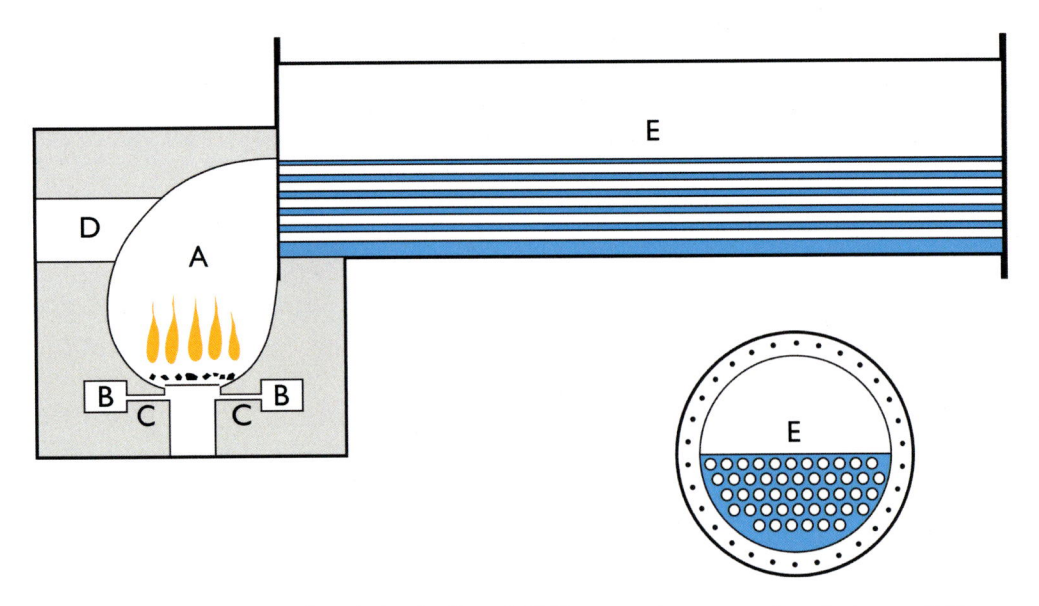

Marc Seguin's patent multi-tubular boiler of 1828, presaging many key features of Henry Booth's boiler for *Rocket*. Firebox (A); tuyères for bellows (B, C); firehole (D); boiler tubes (E). (Andrew Mason)

The *Annales des Ponts et Chaussées* (1831) noted:

> It was Mr Henry Booth ... who suggested the idea to pass the tubes through the boiler; this disposition having the purpose to submit the largest surface area possible to the action of the hot air with the smallest tube area; by these means the heat is rapidly communicated to the water, and does not [immediately] escape in the chimney, an inconvenience noted in the boilers with large tubes. [*Annales des Ponts et Chaussées* (1831): 2]

The wrought iron boiler barrel was 6 feet (1.8 m) long and 3 feet 4 inches (1.0 m) in diameter. It is made from four plates of quarter-inch Staffordshire 'RB rolled iron' lap- and strap-riveted together. Running longitudinally through it are twenty-five copper pipes of 3-inch outside diameter. Because the technology did not yet exist to produce seamless tubes, each boiler tube was individually rolled and soldered. While Booth might have had the idea of the multi-tubular boiler, it was another thing entirely to build it, and considerable difficulty was had in preventing the boiler ends from deflecting under pressure, with Robert Stephenson having to put in additional boiler stays:

> 21 August 1829
> The tubes are all clunk into the Boiler, which is placed on the frame ... the clinking of the tubes is tight with boiling water. I am arranging the hydraulic pump to prove the boiler up to 160lbs before proceeding any further.

> 26 August 1829
> On Wednesday I had the boiler filled with water and put up the pressure of 70lb per square inch when I found that the yielding of the boiler end injured the clinking of the

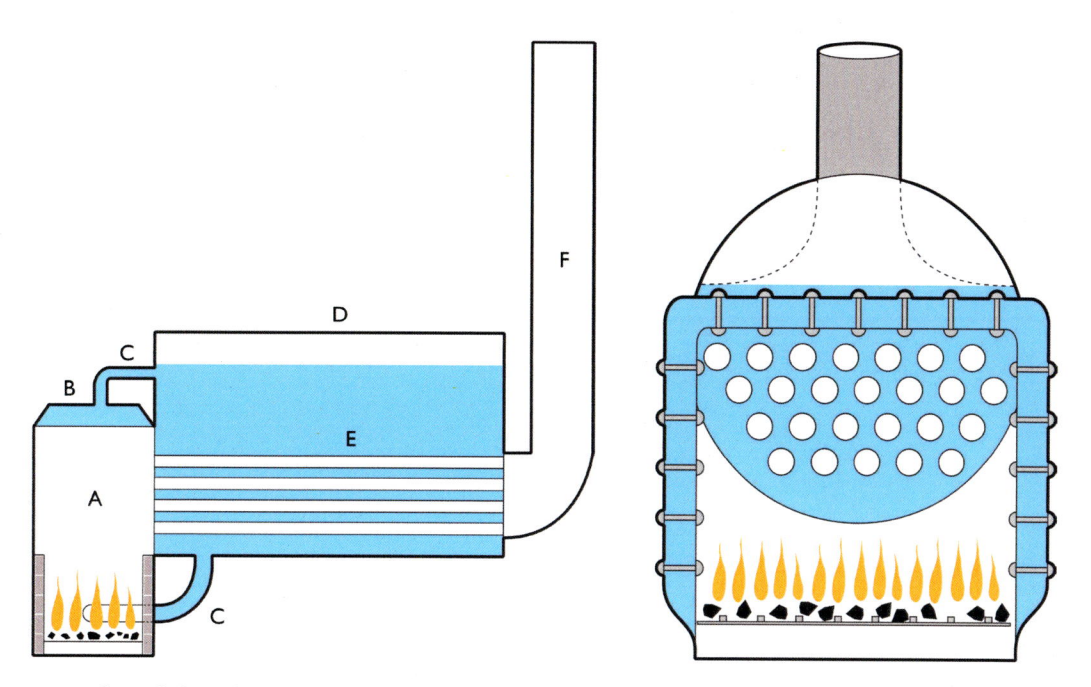

Above left and right: *Rocket*'s multi-tube boiler: hot gasses from the firebox (A) heated the water jacket (B) and passed through the twenty-five copper flue tubes (E). Hot water from the water jacket could circulate with that in the boiler via four pipes (C). (Andrew Mason after John Rastrick)

tubes. I therefore thought it prudent to stop the experiment until we got some more stays put into the boiler.

31 August 1829
After the [additional] stays were put in, we tried the boiler up to 120 lbs. per sq. inch, which I found it necessary to put in two more stays in order to make the ends withstand 150 [i.e. three times working pressure] – this would be totally unnecessary if the fixed pressure for the trial were 120. We can however make it stand the required pressure. [Rail 1008/88/4]

John Rastrick inspected the boiler:

The Body of the Great boiler is three feet four inches diameter and six feet long. Through this boiler there go twenty-five copper tubes, three inches outside diameter, which are fixed into the Boiler at each end in such a way that the highest Row is about three inches below the surface of the water when the Boiler has its full compliment of Water in it.

The Caloric and Heated air from the Fire Place and small Boiler, passes through these tubes into the Chimney which is enlarged at its Bottom to embrace the whole of the five and twenty copper tubes. The chimney is fifteen inches in diameter at the upper part, which is ten feet high above the rail road. [NRM 1945-108]

The revolutionary part of the boiler was a proper firebox, as a self-contained structure rather than being formed at one end of the large boiler flue; Rastrick referred to that on

Rocket as a 'small boiler'. The firebox measured 3 feet by 2 feet, and was made from copper sheet, surrounded by a copper water jacket on three sides. To encourage water flow around the firebox, two copper pipes fed water into the bottom of the water jacket, and two at the top, so that due to convection water was constantly circulating in the hottest part of the boiler. The firebox was made by an outside contractor, and when it arrived was not quite square. To strengthen the firebox, copper stays supported the inner and outer skins. Rastrick described it as:

> A Small Boiler which is constantly kept full of water; this serves as the Fire Place, the grate being three feet wide and two feet long, with an area of six feet, which is 6/10 of a sq.ft. of the grate for each horse power. The surface of this boiler exposed to the action of the fire is eighteen square feet ... The principal objection to this construction, is the difficulty in getting at the inside to clean it out. The sediment of the water will mostly settle to the bottom, into the narrow part where it is riveted together, but the Scurf or Calciferous encrustation will affix itself to all parts of the inside of the boiler. [NRM 1945-108]

To overcome this, it was proposed to 'make a small hole' – i.e. a mud hole – 'on each side, towards the Bottom', but due to the small space available for the hands or any tools, Rastrick

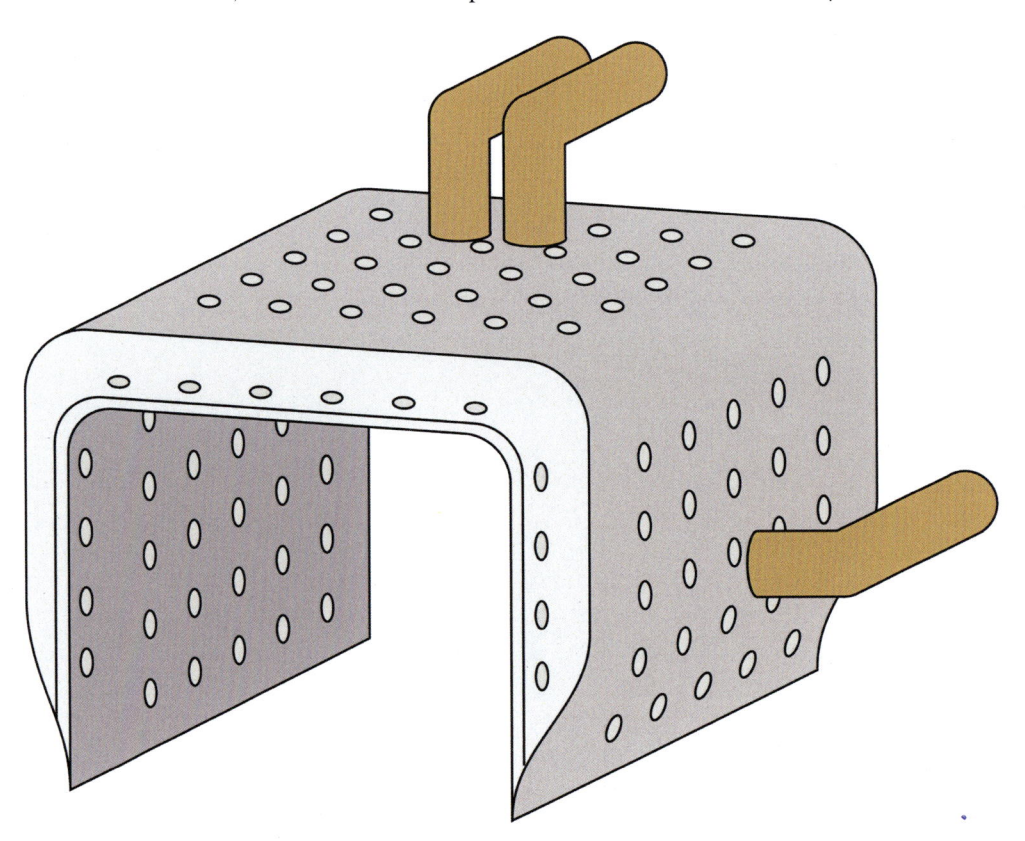

As important as the twenty-five flue tubes passing through the boiler barrel was a separate water-jacketed firebox (the hottest part of the boiler), which allowed good flame development, increasing steam-raising capacity. (Andrew Mason after John Rastrick)

thought 'the withdrawing [of] the sediment will be a tedious and difficult operation'. On the 1979 and 2010 replicas of *Rocket*, the lower copper circulating pipes are removed and washed out, allowing the firebox to be flushed. The multiple copper tubes in the boiler, along with the water-jacketed firebox, combined to give *Rocket* a total heating surface of 135 ¾ square feet (Rastrick), although modern authors have calculated the heating surface to be 138 square feet (42.8 m^2).

Wheels and Motion

One of Robert Stephenson's ambitions when he returned home from South America was to improve the efficiency and appearance of the locomotives built at Forth Street:

> Since I came down from London, I have been talking a great deal to my father about endeavouring to reduce the size and ugliness of our travelling-engines, by applying the steam [cylinders] either on the side of the boiler or beneath it entirely, somewhat similar to Gurney's steam carriage. He has agreed to an alteration which I think will considerably reduce the quantity of machinery, as well as liability to mismanagement. Mr Pease writes my father that in their present complicated state they cannot be managed by 'fools'. Therefore they must undergo some alteration or amendment. [Warren: 143]

He added:

> Accidents are in a great measure under the control of the Enginemen, which are, by the by, not the most manageable class of beings. They perhaps want improvement as much as the engines.

Unlike *Sans Pareil* or *Novelty*, *Rocket* used a 'dog clutch' to enable her to reverse: the famous Robert Stephenson 'flying reverse', part of his rolling programme to improve the efficiency and mechanical simplicity of the locomotive. He wrote that, 'It answers as well as anything possibly can do, and the men like it very much ... it is now as simple as I can make it and I believe effectual.'

The two eccentrics – one per cylinder – sandwiched between two cheek plates are mounted on a sleeve which is free to move from side to side between a pair of collars clamped to the axle. A pedal on the footplate works a yoke, which shifts the eccentrics laterally, engaging a 'driving dog' on the collar into a curved slot on the eccentric cheek plate. The driving dogs are set 90º to each other to provide fore and back gear. The curved slots allow the direction to be changed at relatively high speed, c. 5–7 mph, theoretically giving *Rocket* an advantage over her two rivals. To engage reverse gear, the locomotive had to be slowed by shutting off steam, the pedal on the footplate was depressed, which shifted the eccentrics to the right, engaging the right-hand driving dog. With the locomotive in reverse gear, the regulator could be opened, and the back-pressure in the cylinders used to brake the locomotive or even bring it to a stand and hold it stationary. Despite the 'flying reverse', John Rastrick records that

Left: Detail of *Rocket*'s left-hand driving wheel and connecting rod. Note the two try-cocks in the rather inaccessible position at the front of the boiler. (Matthew Jackson)

Below: Detail of *Rocket*'s right-hand big end: the spherical steel crank pin fits into a brass ball and socket joint, allowing the wheel free movement according to the vagaries of the track. (Matthew Jackson)

Rocket's left-hand cylinder, piston rod and connecting-rod assembly. The steep angle of the cylinders is clearly emphasised in this view. (Matthew Jackson)

the process of slowing down, changing direction and getting up to speed took on average 2 minutes 30 seconds, some 20 seconds slower than *Sans Pareil*, although from Rastrick's figures *Sans Pareil* took longer to get into forward gear than reverse. That *Rocket* was slower to change gear might have been technological – Robert Stephenson noted she didn't run as well in reverse as in forward gear when on trial at Killingworth and perhaps that problem had not yet been solved, or perhaps it was because William Gowland (the driver of *Sans Pareil*) had over a year's experience with the similar valve gear on *Royal George*, whereas Mark Wakefield had been with *Rocket* only a matter of weeks.

The eccentrics feed back to a rocking shaft mounted on the front of the firebox. This rocking shaft, in turn, drives a pair of slide rods, which are fitted with gab-hooks at their footplate ends. These gab hooks drop over pins fitted to the valve handles, which in turn drive the back-head rocking shaft which works the valve spindles. By unhooking these gabs, the valve spindles are disconnected from the eccentrics and the locomotive can be driven 'on the handles', changing the valves by hand to start it. Once the locomotive is running freely, the gabs can be engaged and the locomotive will run by itself.

Above and below: *Rocket*'s eccentric cluster and dog-clutch. A yoke, operated by a pedal on the footplate, slips the eccentrics left or right to engage with the driving dogs, providing fore- and back-gear. (Matthew Jackson/Andrew Mason)

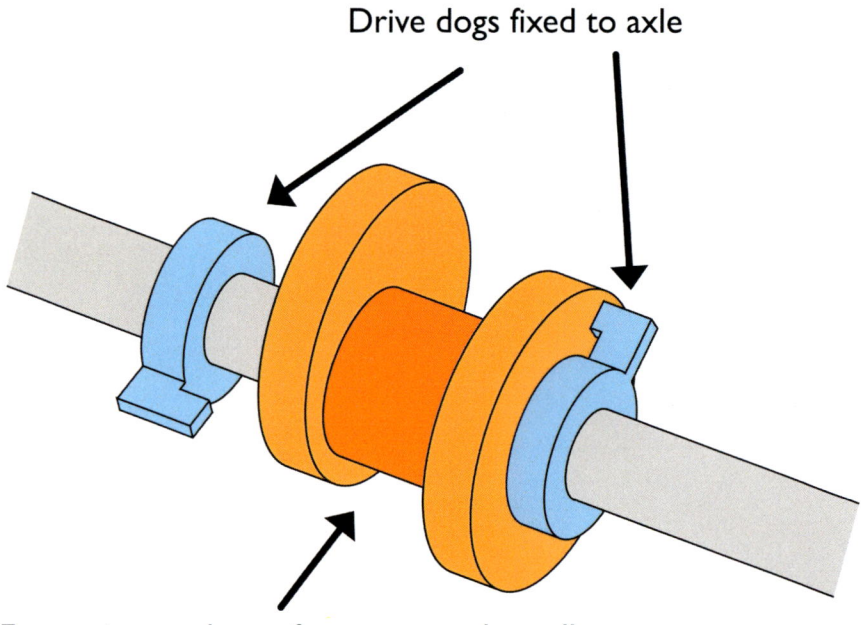

Drive dogs fixed to axle

Eccentrics on sleeve, free to move laterally

Above: Detail of *Rocket*'s valve gear: the eccentrics on the driving axle work a rocking shaft, which in turn drives two side levers which terminate in drop-hooks. (Matthew Jackson)

Right: *Rocket*'s footplate. The valve levers that control the valves are visible on the left, together with the foot-pedal which shifts the eccentrics. For safety reasons the replica is fitted with a modern pressure gauge and gauge glasses. (Lauren Jaye Gradwell)

Testing and Running-In Trials

Rocket was completed by 2 September 1829, but due to the absence of any test track at the Forth Street Works, arrangements were made with Nicholas Wood for *Rocket* to be taken to Killingworth Colliery for running-in trials. Therefore, Wood must have known at least some of the capabilities of *Rocket* before the Trials took place a month later.

Running-in trials took place between 3 and 5 September at Killingworth, with Robert Stephenson reporting to Henry Booth upon their completion, noting the difficulties of firing with coke:

> It appeared prudent to make an actual trial and make any alterations that might present themselves during an experiment of that kind. The fire burns admirably and abundance of steam is raised when the fire is carefully attended to. This is an essential point because a coke fire when let down is bad to get up again; this rather prevented our experiment being so successful as it would have been throughout. [RAIL 1008/88/4]

The running-in trials also found problems with the valve gear and their operation, but *Rocket* managed to achieve speeds higher than that specified in the Trial rules:

> We also found that from the construction of the working gear that the Engine did not work so well in one direction as in the other; this will be remedied. We started from Killingworth Pit, with five wagons weighing four Tuns. Add to this the tender and 40 men we proceeded up an ascent 11 or 12 feet per Mile at 8 Miles per hour.
>
> We went three Miles on this Railway – on a level part laid with Malleable Iron rail, we attained a speed of 12 Miles an hour and ... I believe the steam did not sink on this part. On the whole, the Engine is capable of doing as much if not more than set forth in the stipulations. [RAIL 1008/88/4]

Stephenson also took the opportunity to fine-tune *Rocket*'s exhaust system. Exhaust steam from both cylinders passed along copper 'Eduction Pipes' to the base of the chimney, thus creating a partial vacuum drawing the hot gasses from the fire through the tubes. The existing exhaust design had not been successful and as a result Robert Stephenson carried out a series of experiments with different diameters of coned blast pipes (one per 'Eduction Pipe'). A letter written to *The Engineer* in September 1883 suggests that it was Henry Booth who suggested to Robert Stephenson that he 'turn the exhaust up into the chimney' through a coned-nozzle rather than just open ended 'eduction pipes' doing away with the need for bellows to 'liven up the fire'. The often abrasive John Wesley Hackworth (Chapter 3) claimed that Stephenson stole the idea:

> Mr Stephenson, being anxious to investigate Sanspareil's blast pipe, dispatched a nocturnal visitant to inspect it, and take its dimensions. Our informant on this little bit of *finesse* is the actual person who made the survey: he is still living. [*The Engineer*, 14 August 1857]

J. W. Hackworth also believed that his father had a guard posted over *Sans Pareil* to prevent any more of her 'secrets' being stolen! This 'battle of the blast pipe' resulted in a lengthy and often acrimonious correspondence in the pages of *The Engineer* during 1857. Robert Stephenson, writing to Samuel Smiles in the 1850s, noted that *Rocket* had two blast pipes (one per eduction pipe) and that it was the coning of the blast pipe orifice that was important to the operation of the blast pipe.

Robert Stephenson certainly knew technical details of *Sans Pareil*, however; his firm was responsible for casting and boring her cylinders. He described *Sans Pareil* in a letter to Henry Booth on 21 August 1829, including the design of the boiler and valve gear. Of *Rocket*'s twin blast pipes, Robert Stephenson recalled in 1858:

> A series of experiments were made ... their efficiency was tested by the amount of vacuum that was formed in the smoke box. The degree of rarefaction was determined by

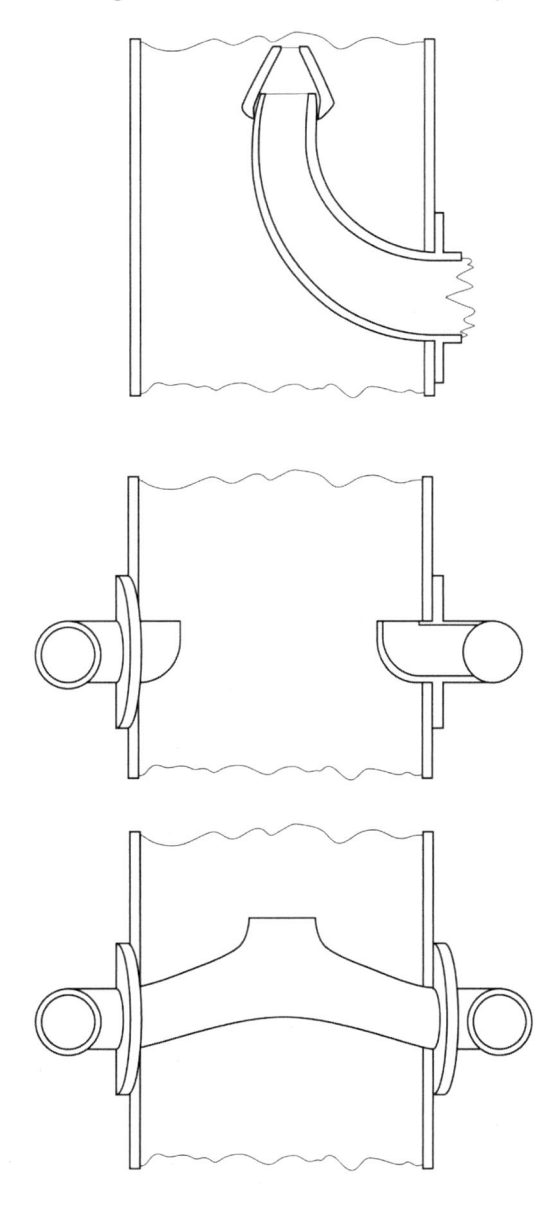

Top: *Sans Pareil*'s single, coned, blastpipe: centre *Rocket*'s twin 'eduction pipes'; bottom *Rocket*'s modified exhaust arrangement. (Andrew Mason after Richard Roberts)

a glass tube fixed to the bottom of the smoke-box and descending into a bucket of water, - the tube being open at both ends. As the rarefaction took place the water would of course rise in the tube ... These experiments certainly showed that a considerable increase of draught was obtained by contracting the orifice, and accordingly the two blast-pipes in the Rocket were contracted to slightly below the area of the steam ports ... The Rocket worked perfectly well with the double blast-pipe, and to the best of my recollection, the prize was won without any alteration having been made in that part of the engine. [S. Smiles: 502]

Following Rainhill, Nicholas Wood states that *Rocket* was fitted with a single rather than double blast-pipe because, in Robert Stephenson's opinion, a single blast-pipe took up less space. He thus probably appears to have been unaware that the change from a double- to single-blast pipe with a narrow exit would increase the draught and therefore generation of steam. Richard Roberts (1789–1864) – of Sharp, Roberts & Co., Manchester – writing in *The Engineer* (31 July 1857) stated that before this alteration, *Rocket* was 'unable to generate steam for more than fifteen miles per hour', and that the 'immediate consequence' of fitting the single blast-pipe was that 'the draft was increased ... trebled, and the speed of the engine augmented from fifteen miles per hour with barely sufficient steam, to thirty with an abundance of that necessary article'.

Rocket to Rainhill

Rocket was dismantled in Newcastle, and left the Forth Street works at '4 o'clock on Saturday afternoon, the 12th day of September', arriving at Carlisle by canal on 'the Monday afternoon following at 2 o'clock'. From Carlisle, *Rocket* was transferred to a coastal lighter 'lying in the Canal Basin, and conveyed to Boness, and there put on board the 'Cumberland' steamer', which took it to Liverpool, arriving on Friday 18 September. Carts and wagons were used to transport the various parts of *Rocket* from Liverpool Docks to the workshops at Crown Street Yard.

Sent with *Rocket* were Ralph Hutchinson and Mark Wakefield, formerly an apprentice of Stephenson & Co.; Ralph Hutchinson later became 'principal foreman' while William Hutchinson (d. 1853) was the 'extremely able and active' Forth Street Works Manager:

Ralph Hutchinson, of Newcastle-upon-Tyne, assisted to construct *The Rocket* at that place, and attended it to Liverpool, where he was invested with the management of it by the late Mr Robert Stephenson, with Mark Wakefield as his assistant, and Robert Hope as fireman, Ralph Hutchinson being at all times responsible for the efficient working order of the engine. [*Bell's Weekly Messenger*, 29 November 1851]

John Rowland, a former Stephenson & Co. employee, also describes Mark Wakefield and Robert Hope as *Rocket*'s crew at Rainhill. Wakefield was among the earliest drivers on the Liverpool & Manchester, and together with John Dunn and Robert Hope, he 'ballasted with the *Lancashire Witch*' while 'the works were still in progress'. Robert Stannard – son of the contactor for the Chat Moss section – recalled later in life:

> In the evening, after the first days' trials were made, Mr Stephenson came to my father, "Now Stannard, let us have a trip to ourselves." whereupon he got up, followed by Wakefield the Driver and my father, Mr [Henry] Booth, Mr [John] Moss and myself. There was not much room, and Mr Stephenson remarked, "Put your boy up on the tub, Stannard; he'll be more out of harm's way." And there indeed I sat during my first ride on the *Rocket*. [*The Engineer*, 17 October 1884]

Unfortunately, there was difficulty re-assembling *Rocket* at Crown Street as the carrying wheels set under the firebox were found not to fit. Stannard, again:

> The *Rocket* was put together in the Edge Hill Engine Sheds, only just before the day of the trials ... and the pair of trailing wheels under the fire-box ... only arrived the day before [the trials began]. When these wheels were placed under the frame, it was found, to the great annoyance of the erectors, that the journals were too large to fit the bearings. It was impossible to get them altered in time for the trial; but the difficulty was overcome by substituting a pair of cast iron wheels from a tip wagon, with square-ended axles ... at the last moment; and on these she ran at the Rainhill Trials. [*The Engineer*, 17 October 1884]

Rocket, accompanied by one of the coaches built for *Lion* in 1930, raising steam outside the Power Hall in Manchester, 2005. (David Boydell)

Rocket and her coachload of 1830s passengers steams over Water Street Bridge, September 2005. (David Boydell)

These substitute wheels were recorded by Rastrick as being 2 feet 8½ inches in diameter, some 2½ inches larger than those they temporarily replaced. It was at Crown Street that *Rocket* received its final coat of paint and her name: up until this point she had been known as 'The Premium Engine'. Her canary-yellow colour, according to Nathaniel Worsdell (who built *Rocket*'s tender), was chosen by George Stephenson. In the early nineteenth century yellow generally signified speed, and indeed it was the colour of the fastest, crack stagecoaches. Thus in painting *Rocket* yellow, Stephenson was saying to the spectators 'this is a fast engine' – the nineteenth-century equivalent of painting it red (all red cars go fast thanks to Mr Ferrari) or with go-faster stripes. The name was also deliberate: while it has been suggested *Rocket* was named after the often unreliable invention of William Congreve Jr, in a period when the steam locomotive was dangerous and generally believed to be prone to explosions, naming *Rocket* after a weapon of war might not necessarily have been such a good public relations move. It is more likely that *Rocket* was named after one of the most fashionable stagecoaches of the day, 'The Rocket', which ran only during the summer season, carrying well-to-do fashionable persons from London to Brighton. In 1829, 'The Rocket' was considered the fastest road coach of the day, with an average speed of 10 mph. Thus, to the visitors from London, the name *Rocket*, and its colour, would have been familiar. In trying to win over a sceptical public to this new mode of transportation, George Stephenson was drawing on familiar colours and names, as if to say, 'My engine is just as fast, and safe as the best stagecoach.' In fact, the paint on *Rocket* was not even dry at Rainhill; Robert Stannard recalled when he had his ride on *Rocket*, he was 'literally stuck on' as the '[water] butt had only been newly painted the day before.' *Rocket* did not retain her yellow colour scheme for long: she was repainted dark green before the opening day (15 September 1830) and indeed the oldest layer of paint on the surviving locomotive is dark green. The two other contenders also shared names with famous stagecoaches: the 'Sans Pareil' ran from Liverpool to Hull and the 'Novelty' was popular with travellers from London to Birmingham.

Rocket Under Trial

Rocket's trial was set for Thursday 8 October 1829. She had been weighed at Rainhill and judged to be 2 tons 12 cwt 1 qr on the driving wheels and 1 ton 2 cwt 3 qr on the carrying wheels, making a total of 4 tons 5 cwt. Robert Stephenson had estimated her to weigh

Rocket roars past *Planet* at speed on the Great Central Main Line; note the charring of paint on the chimney due to high exhaust temperatures. (Matthew Jackson)

73

(empty) 4 tons (80 cwt), and 4 tons 5 cwt 1 qr in working order. The tender, with a full compliment of coke and water, weighed 3 tons 4 cwt 2 lbs.

John Rastrick was on hand to observe the fire being laid in *Rocket*'s firebox and the time taken to raise full boiler pressure (50 psi). He recorded the tender was carrying 300 gallons of water together with 8 cwt 3 qrs 2 lbs of coke. The fire was lit at 9.37 a.m. precisely, and steam was raised 57 minutes later, at 10.34 a.m.; Nicholas Wood observed that *Rocket* was actually 'blowing off at 50psi'. She had burned 1 cwt 1 qr 2 lbs of coke. Stephenson, Hutchinson, Wakefield and Hope fussed around her. With her safety valve blowing, *Rocket* steamed off at 10:36.50 to her destiny.

Drawing a load of 12 tons 5 cwt (three times her weight), *Rocket* took 1 minute 25 seconds to get up to full speed by the first post, which she passed at 10:38.15, and passed the second post where Nicholas Wood was stationed at 10:45.58: a respectable, but not record shattering speed of 11.6 mph. As Mark Wakefield warmed to his task, speed gradually rose from 12.4 mph to 14.5 mph and finally, on her ninth trip, 21.4 mph. Following the tenth trip, there was a 'pit-stop' of 14 minutes 34 seconds to take on water and coke and to oil round: 'During this time the steam was blowing off and the fuel wasting.'

Rocket re-started at 14:02.12 (by Rastrick's watch). Flushed with enthusiasm, speeds rose from 13 mph to 15 mph and with a final flourish *Rocket* reached 24.1 mph. The oft-quoted statement by Nicholas Wood that *Rocket* achieved a speed of 29 mph is incorrect; he simply got his maths wrong. While not the fastest locomotive on trial, *Rocket* had run comfortably faster than the stipulated minimum, and had done so almost continuously, and under load, for 70 miles – perhaps the greatest distance a steam locomotive had ever run. Furthermore, she had done so without any mishap, accident or mechanical failure. The *Mechanics' Magazine*, usually antagonistic to Messrs Stephenson, believed that:

> Whatever may be the merits of The Rocket, as contrasted with either of its rivals, it is so much superior to the old locomotive engines in use, as to entitle Mr R Stephenson to the most marked and liberal consideration. If a Parliamentary Reward of a large amount was justly conferred on Harrison [for his chronometer to aid navigation at sea] ... the Directors of the Liverpool & Manchester Railway cannot do wrong in awarding Mr Stephenson a premium of 500l., for producing an engine which has done what no locomotive engine ever before accomplished, gone 70 miles continuously, at an average rate of about 12 miles per hour, with a load three times its own weight attached to it; which has realized a degree of speed and power, which, though much desired, had scarcely been anticipated by the most sanguine ... The Rocket has eclipsed all other locomotive engines.
> [*Mechanics' Magazine*, 24 October 1829]

After the cessation of Rainhill, additional trials were held with *Rocket* on the Whiston Incline where it was found that *Rocket* could haul a load of 8 tons up the 1:96 gradient at 16 mph. A second experiment with a load of 12 tons was performed at the speed of 12½ mph. The *Annales des Ponts et Chaussées* (1831) therefore refuted the claim of Rastrick and Walker, who had reported that a locomotive could not ascend so steep an incline: 'These experiments were made to show the palpable error of Mr Walker, these experiments and their direct application, have decided this issue.' Despite this apparent success at hill climbing, *Rocket*'s driver, Mark Wakefield, recalled later in life:

I [Mark Wakefield] were driver of the famous "Rocket" locomotive-engine ... when we came to the Incline, we'd stop her; tie down the safety valve and build up the fire. We'd set her off and run her up, running along behind 'til she gained the top.

Further trials took place on 19 October over the Rainhill Level: in the first experiment *Rocket* made six out-and-back runs, with a load of 36 tons (including the tender), at an average speed of 13 mph. Runs with a load of 40 tons were performed at 13½ mph and a final run with a load of 45 tons at 13¼ mph. From these experiments, the *Annales des Ponts et Chaussées* concluded that *Rocket*, with a load of 20 tons of goods or passengers, could comfortably run at an average speed of 13 mph between Liverpool and Manchester.

Rocket looking at home at Liverpool Road with her short passenger train of replica L&M second- and first-class coaches. (Matthew Jackson)

Chapter 5

After Rainhill

The three judges met on 16 October, concluding that *Rocket* was the winner of the Rainhill Trials and the £500 premium was awarded to her builders. The directors of the Liverpool & Manchester therefore ordered four *Rocket*-type locomotives from Robert Stephenson & Co. on 26 October, for delivery in January 1830.

There was considerable recrimination after the trials; Hackworth's supporters complained that the whole thing had been an 'inside job', that the Trial Stipulations had been written

The Rainhill Trials were re-staged at the Llangollen Railway for BBC *Timewatch* in 2002. All three replica competitors are on shed, being prepared. (Matthew Jackson)

Sans Pareil replica raising steam at Llangollen, 2002. (Matthew Jackson)

only after the judges (and directors) had seen *Rocket* and *Novelty* running under steam, and, suggested the *Mechanics' Magazine*, had been written in such a way that only *Rocket* could fulfil them. William Kitching, one of the Stockton & Darlington Railway Committee members, expressed similar sentiments in a letter to Hackworth:

Darlington, 17th of the 10th month 1829.
I should have been extremely glad to have heard that fair play had been allowed to the different engine makers ... From what I have heard of the doings with you, the Engine which had a Booth as the inventor of the copper pipes in the boiler was, without either judge or jury, to be the winner. [*The Engineer*, 14 August 1857]

One correspondent to the *Liverpool Mercury* added:

Respecting the recent series of experiments on the Rail-Way at Rainhill, I take the liberty of expressing my dissent ... and particularly where it is stated that the Directors "have had the advantage of some of the ablest Mechanics in the Kingdom." The truth is, however, that so little publicity was given to the proposals, and so economical were they that few either knew of them, or would risk the great expense of constructing a locomotive machinery on such terms. Had sufficient inducement been held out, by proposing to pay at least all the expenses of three or four of the most meritorious machines ...
The Directors and their Engineer wrote their rules and organised their experiments in such a way that only one locomotive-engine could ever fulfill the requirements. That machine being that of Mr Stephenson and Booth ...

Several Objections should have been made as to the Mode of the Experiments, and to the Judge and Jury, as offered by the Directors, as several important points are still in doubt. [*Liverpool Mercury*, 30 October 1829]

Hackworth wrote to the directors of the Liverpool & Manchester, asking for a retrial and seeking financial recompense for his engine. He noted that the 'the defects were of a nature easily to be remedied' and could have been done at Rainhill. As a result, the directors agreed to a further trial on the Rainhill Level, but because the famous Skew Bridge was then under construction, *Sans Pareil* could only run over three-quarters of a mile of the original course. She arrived at Rainhill on 25 October and was lit up the following day:

At half-past ten o'clock, one of your Agents weighed in 7cwt of Fuel – the engine was kept continunally in motion (save watering) til 6 at night, when a Portion of the fuel remained unconsumed – during the day the Engine ascended and descended the Inclined Plane repeatedly, with water and fuel and twelve passengers (at the agreed rate [i.e. 10mph]). Afterwards a load of 38 tons was attached to the Engine – also 15 Passengers – thus laden up an ascent (this I am informed) of 4ft. pr mile the speed maintained was 13 ½ miles per hour – during the Day the fire was never cleaned. [NRM HACK 1-1-25]

Hackworth also demanded a re-match of the three contenders, so long as 'the Engines are altered back to their then state' and offered to forfeit *Sans Pareil* if 'it did not in every way exceed anything performed on the day of trial, say a minimum of ... 60 tons

Sans Pareil, accompanied by L&M No. 57 *Lion* and a replica first-class coach, at 'Rocket 150' in May 1980.

78

at 10 miles pr. Hour'. The directors declined the rematch but did purchase *Sans Pareil* for £550, the price asked for by Hackworth.

Sans Pareil was then moved to the Bolton & Leigh Railway for a further series of trials there, tackling the Daubhill and Chequerbent Inclines:

> Up the first, a mile and a half long, the "Sans Pareil" drew its tender with coke and water, two loaded wagons and a carriage containing passengers – making a train load of 15 tons – at an average speed of nine miles an hour. On the steeper incline, with a load of 4 tons 15 cwts., the speed was from 9 to 11 miles per hour. [NRM HACK 1-1-25]

The *Manchester Mercury* reported on 8 December 1829 that another trial of *Sans Pareil* had taken place:

> An Experiment has been tried on the Bolton and Leigh Railway, with the locomotive engine constructed by Mr Ackworth of Darlington, and the result far exceeded the most sanguine expectations of that gentleman. He had never entertained the idea that the Engine could ascend the inclined plane, which, however, was accomplished in about 3 1/2 minutes, the distance being upwards of three quarters of a mile, and the ascent being one in thirty. On its arrival at the top, a number of waggons were attached, these were instantly filled with persons, and the engine was covered with passengers, amounting to at least one hundred in all. With this load it proceeded at a rate of 16 to 18 miles an hour.

Sans Pareil was subsequently sold to John Hargreaves, the lessee of the Bolton & Leigh Railway, for a mere £110. The *Liverpool Mercury* reported on Friday 9 April 1830:

> Bolton & Leigh Railway. On Tuesday ... the Sans Pareil engine went, with coach attached to it, and adapted for Passengers, went from Bolton to Leigh, attended by some of the Directors of the Company. On its return from the former place to Bolton, it ran, using the lower incline next to Leigh, at a rate of fifteen miles per hour, and at the higher incline at Chowbent, at the rate of eight miles an hour. The engine, including stoppages came from Leigh to Bolton in thirty-five minutes. The distance between the two is estimated to be eight miles by the rail-road.

One Manchester newspaper thought *Sans Pareil* 'ugly and ill-adapted' for its new rôle, while a Newcastle 'paper described her as 'neat, and compact'. *Sans Pareil* worked on the Bolton & Leigh Railway until 1844 when she was purchased by John Hick of Bolton and used as a pumping engine for the next nineteen years. Hick 'restored' her and presented *Sans Pareil* to the Patent Office Museum (now the Science Museum) in 1864.

It was not only supporters of *Sans Pareil* who felt aggrieved: so too did those of *Novelty*, who claimed that *Rocket* had been running at a boiler pressure of 70 psi! Analysis by Rastrick showed this claim to be false (*Rocket* had indeed worked at 50 psi), concluding that *Novelty* was 'enormously deficient in power'. Davidson and Glitheroe (2006) agree with Rastrick's conclusion, arguing that *Novelty* was under-powered because most of the power generated was lost driving the blowing apparatus: the cylinders could deliver 6 hp, but the blower required 6.5 hp to work it! To overcome this loss of power, a third cylinder was added to drive the blower and *Novelty* underwent additional trials during spring 1830:

> The Novelty, which has been materially improved by the alterations it has undergone, was exercised on the railway at Rainhill. It is stated to have drawn 31 tons gross at a speed of 12 miles an hour; the distance traversed was a mile and a half. A supplementary cylinder has been added to this engine, for the sole purpose of blowing the bellows, and the two cylinders are independent of each other. [*Lancaster Gazette*, 2 January 1830]

Another newspaper reported how

> The Novelty Steam-Carriage, having undergone a thorough repair at Liverpool, has re-appeared on the Railway, and has been tried sometimes with, and sometimes without a load. When so heavy a load as thirty-five tons - ten times the weight of the carriage - was put on, it proceeded at the rate of twelve miles per hour; but when the load was light, and consisted only of passengers, it advanced at the extraordinary rate of thirty five miles in one hour! Nothing can be more smooth and easy than the entire action of this carriage; all the mechanics and working are hidden out of sight; all its parts work in harmony with each other. [*Cork Constitution*, 2 January 1830]

Trials under the supervision of Robert Daglish Jnr took place on 26 January 1830: with a load of 28.5 tons *Novelty* ran at an average speed of 8 mph, and burned 84 lbs of coke an hour. With her improved steam-powered blowing apparatus, *Novelty*

> Carried nearly ten times its own weight, with the adhesion of only two wheels, which is certainly something extraordinary, thought I am aware it will not do it in all seasons of the year. [NRM 1945-108]

Success of the *Novelty* during these trials led to the *Mechanics' Magazine* stating that 'the superiority of "the blast principle" [i.e. use of forced air blast rather than a blast pipe] – a recent invention of Messrs. Braithwaite and Ericsson – is beyond doubt'. The further trials of *Novelty* did not pass without incident; the *Leeds Mercury* (14 January 1830) reported that 'a person named Tollerton' attempted to 'jump in the waggon' but in so doing, slipped and fell 'and instantly the ponderous machine passed over his head'. The *Mercury* delighted in informing its readers that Tollerton's head was 'crushed to atoms! The whole was an act of a moment'.

From the apparent success with *Novelty*, Braithwaite and Ericsson 'positively contracted' to build two engines 'not exceeding 5 tons weight, and capable of drawing 40 tons gross, at a rate of 18 miles an hour' burning no more than 'half a pound weight [of coke] per mile'. The engines were to cost £1,000 each and be ready by 15 June 1830. With Royal permission the pair were named *William IV* and *Queen Adelaide*. The boiler for *William IV* was a joint patent between Braithwaite, Ericsson, Vignoles and Alexander Nimmo. Because of their ongoing legal case, a large fan, driven by exhausted steam and mounted on top of the boiler, spinning at 52 mph, was used to induct a draught through the fire. Although Braithwaite and Ericsson had promised delivery in June, *William IV*

Both of *Novelty*'s cylinders were presented to John Melling, the L&M's foreman of the locomotives. One is incorporated in the Science Museum replica, while this, the second, is preserved at Rainhill Library.

was not delivered until late August. Trials in September ended in near disaster when she de-railed and nearly fell down the embankment near the Sankey Viaduct. After further modifications, formal trials in February 1831 showed she struggled to make steam – at one point having to be towed home by a Stephenson engine. Late in life, Ericsson described *William IV* and *Queen Adelaide* as 'very classical' in appearance, but like *Novelty*, 'miserably inefficient': the *Manchester Courier* (28 August 1830) noted that during trials that summer, *William IV* 'did not answer the expectations of the gentlemen'. One correspondent to the *Register of Arts* concluded:

> The gentlemen who had the honour of petitioning our beloved sovereign for permission to call these engines *King William IV* and *Queen Adelaide*, may be proud of the appropriate choice, as kings and queens are seldom known to work, and these appear no exception to the Royal rule. [*Register of Arts* (1832): 23]

Despite the unfailing support of the *Mechanics' Magazine*, both of these locomotives were failures. Many thought that the claims of Braithwaite and Ericsson had been 'so exaggerated, so wonderfully puffed up, and the public exceedingly gulled' by the *Mechanics' Magazine* and other anti-Stephenson journals. Luke Hebert, editor of the *Register of Arts*, concluded: 'Messrs Braithwaite and Ericsson may indeed congratulate themselves in having ... influential advocates in the editors of "The Liverpool Mercury" and "The London Mechanics' Magazine."' (*Register of the Arts*, vol. IV, 1830).

A war of words erupted between the *Mechanics' Magazine* and the Manchester newspapers: the *Manchester Guardian* was blamed for spreading pro-Stephenson 'falsehoods'. In reply, the *Manchester Guardian* took up cudgels against the little 'knot of

A sketch of Braithwaite & Ericsson's larger, but even less successful, forced-draught locomotive *William IV*. Rather than a bellows blowing under the fire, a fan was mounted on top of the firebox. 'All very classical, but hopelessly inefficient.'

pseudo-mechanics' from the *Mechanics' Magazine* who had done everything in their power to detract from Robert Stephenson's achievements. The *Guardian* hoped that the failure of *William IV* had proved once and for all that the Stephenson-type was the superior machine.

William IV and *Queen Adelaide* were sold to the St Helens & Runcorn Gap Railway as ballast engines. *Novelty* languished 'in a corner of the warehouses at Manchester, forsaken and neglected'. She was rebuilt in 1833 by Robert Daglish Jnr with a new multi-tubular boiler, new cylinders and wheels. Her wheels and cylinders were presented to John Melling, the latter being used to drive machinery in his ironworks.

Whither *Rocket*?

What was in store for the victor? Immediately after the Trials, *Rocket* was taken to Liverpool, where it was involved in a number of 'Public Relations Exercises', running short trips along the as yet uncompleted line. A fortnight after the Trials, *Rocket* was recorded by the *Liverpool Mercury* (6 November 1829) as on 'Thursday last' having

> Drawn the still more astonishing load of 42 tons, or ten times its own weight, at the rate of 14 miles an hour, which is by far the greatest task that has ever been performed by a locomotive ...
>
> Another class of experiments was afterwards tried in order to ascertain with what load, and at what rate, it would ascend the inclined plane at Huyton, when it was found that with 14 tons it travelled the mile and a half ... at 16 miles an hour, and with 16 tons at ... 12 ½ miles an hour.

'See the Conquering Hero Comes': *Rocket* steams triumphantly past the assembled crowd at Bold Colliery, May 1980.

The *Mercury* concluded by adding:

> These performances far exceed the warmest anticipations of the friends of locomotives ... and afford additional and incontestable evidence of their superiority to all modes of conveyance which at present exist.

The Liverpool & Manchester directors advertised on 6 November that *Rocket* would be on show at Rainhill at one o'clock that afternoon. The *Leeds Mercury* reported on Thursday 26 November 1829 that:

> The Manchester and Liverpool Railway was last week visited by a great number of Fashionables. The Rocket Locomotive was again tried and went at times at a rate of 28 miles an hour; average velocity 22 ½ miles; Messrs. Braithwaite and Erickson's carriage is repaired, and will be tried today.

Two days later, the *Manchester Courier* (28 November 1829) reported:

> The superior Powers of the locomotive engine The Rocket were again exhibited, the carriages frequently going at the rate of 28 miles an hour, including the inclined plane at Huyton 22 ½ miles an hour – There have been no experiments with Braithwaite and Erickson's engine, the Novelty, this week, but the repairs are now nearly completed; the engine, it is expected, will be exhibited during the ensuing week. We understand that the experiments made in Mr Fawcett's foundry yard fully justify all the expectations of the proprietors as to the capabilities of the engine.

But not everyone was impressed with the new-fangled 'steam carriages': one McCann was brought before the Salford Magistrates at the New Bailey Prison on Thursday 26 October for 'maliciously' and 'wilfully attempting to overturn the locomotive carriage' *Rocket* near Cross Lane, Manchester, by placing several timber railway sleepers across the track. McCann was fined £5 but 'as he declared that he was not prepared to pay that sum' he was sentenced to two months' imprisonment.

These 'Exhibition' trips were not only good public relations exercises in winning sceptics over to the new railway, but also good for the finances of the company, shares jumping in price from £18 before Rainhill to £175 by the end of November. After these PR trips, *Rocket* had to earn her keep and had the far less glamorous task of working construction trains on the Chat Moss contract. The local press estimated she was saving the contractors at least £50 per month in horses, fodder and men. As soon as one line of rails was laid across the Moss, *Rocket* was used to prove to the doubters and sceptics that a locomotive and train could be run over it, and did so on New Year's Day 1830:

> Mr Stephenson's loco-motive engine, the Rocket ... The Engine passed westwards to Berry [sic, Bury] Lane, near Leigh, over the whole extent of the Moss, a distance of four miles and a half, with a large train attached of wagons and passengers, in seventeen minutes; and returned at a speed amounting to twenty-four miles an hour, but diminished at pleasure where the road was incomplete. The Experiment had the effect of completely proving the

solidity of the work on a part where it was asserted by many engineers that a foundation could never be obtained. [*Manchester Courier*, 2 January 1830]

Rocket 'crossed and re-crossed the Moss' but, on the final return run toward Manchester, near Eccles, she was 'thrown off the road' while travelling 'at a rate of twenty-four miles an hour' when one of her iron carrying wheels broke. The 'water carriage' and 'some of the wagons' were derailed but none of the 'forty individuals riding in and upon the wagons ... received the slightest hurt'. It appears that *Rocket*'s carrying wheel-set was already damaged. One newspaper noted the broken wheel had 'been previously injured by a carriage purposely thrown off the railway' while another commented that the axle of the carrying wheel-set was bent and that *Rocket* had been 'incautiously' put back in service. Was this the result of McCann's attempt to 'wilfully ... overturn a steam carriage' in late October 1829? *Rocket* was, however, speedily repaired:

Immediately after the accident a fresh wheel was substituted for that which was broken, and in three quarters of an hour, the engine was again started, and performed its work with accustomed facility. [*Manchester Courier*, 2 January 1830]

The experiments were continued the following day (2 January), *Rocket* drawing a load of 35 tons 'with which there was not the least sinking' into the Moss. *Rocket* was involved in further experiments on the Moss in April 1830 when she hauled a load of 45 tons, 'this being by far the greatest weight that has yet been conveyed across the Moss', where 'only a few years ago man and horse feared to tread'. During this run *Rocket* attained a maximum speed of 16 mph. *Rocket* was then used in further PR trips during the summer of 1830 in the lead-up to the Grand Opening that September, before returning to construction duties on the Chat Moss section in October. While on the Moss, *Rocket* was involved in her second fatal accident that year: Henry Hunter, a local publican who had developed a habit, 'despite the repeated remonstrations of the Engineer', of hitching a ride on her tender from Ordsall Lane to Eccles, was killed. As *Rocket* was propelling the train back to Manchester, one of the tender wheels broke, throwing Hunter from his perch. He was 'killed on the spot' by the 300-gallon water cask falling on him and crushing him. His body 'presented a horrid spectacle' and was taken to Eccles (where Huskisson had been taken only a month before).

Rocket was obsolete by New Year 1830, when the first of the improved 'Rocket type' locomotives (No. 2 *Arrow*, No. 3 *Wildfire* aka *Meteor*, No. 4 *Dart*, No. 5 *Comet*) locomotives were delivered. They incorporated lessons learned from *Rocket* including cylinders lowered from 38 to 8 degrees, larger driving wheels (5-foot diameter), an increased number of smaller boiler tubes, an internal steam pipe and a steam dome. *Rocket* had been built to do one job: to win the Rainhill Trials. Because *Rocket* was so underpowered compared to the later locomotives, she does not appear to have been used much in revenue-earning service, primarily being used on ballast duties and as a 'pilot engine', running ahead of the train in the dark to ensure no obstacles had been placed on the line. In autumn 1832 she was loaned to the Wigan Branch Railway, and in 1833 designated as a 'stand-by engine' for use in case of emergency. She was used as the testbed for Lord Dundonald's 'Rotary Engine' in 1833 and then laid up at the Edge Hill workshops until being sold to the Earl of Carlisle in October 1836 for use on his colliery railway.

A (non-working) replica of *Rocket* was built by the London & North Western Railway at Crewe in 1881, as part of the Stephenson Centenary.

Chapter 6

Conclusion

Rocket won the Rainhill Trials convincingly: it was the only locomotive left standing at the end of the competition, *Novelty* having been withdrawn and *Sans Pareil* suffering from mechanical faults and the ignominy of the three judges declaring it unfit for purpose. This can be attributed to the fact that *Rocket* was the only locomotive to have had any running-in trials (or indeed, to have run before the Trials took place). Clearly, however, *Rocket* was the more reliable and efficient locomotive, thanks to the design of its boiler and firebox.

'Riot of Steam' in 2005 saw perhaps the largest gathering of early locomotives: replicas of *Rocket* and *Sans Pareil* are joined by *Lion*, the only surviving Liverpool & Manchester locomotive. (David Boydell)

Boiler Capacity

The boiler of *Rocket*, and probably that of *Sans Pareil*, was designed based on two principles outlined by one of the Rainhill judges, Nicholas Wood:

- One square foot of heating surface (30.48 cm^2) will evaporate 20 lb (9 kg) or 2 gallons (9 litres) of water per hour.
- For every horsepower required, a heating surface of 12 square feet (3.65 m^2) was needed.

Rocket was estimated by Rastrick to be 10 hp, although Robert Stephenson later (1830) stated she was 12 hp. Thus, based on Wood's calculations, *Rocket* needed a heating surface of 120 sq. ft (36.57 m^2). Therefore her heating surface of 138 sq. ft (42.8 m^2) was more than sufficient, suggesting a power output of 11 hp. It is likely *Rocket* was designed to be able to work comfortably at 10 hp with sufficient power held in reserve. John Rastrick suggests a maximum power output of 12 hp: at 50 psi each of *Rocket*'s cylinders was capable of producing 6.25 hp, running at a speed of 10 mph. At 20 psi *Rocket* was capable of 10 hp.

According to Wood's theory, therefore, *Rocket*'s heating surface could have generated 2,760 lbs of steam per hour. The success of the boiler design was due to the separate water-jacketed firebox: Daniel Gooch (1816–89) and others demonstrated that the firebox (being the hottest part) generated most of the steam in a locomotive boiler. Most authors, however, have put this figure much lower: one contemporary French observer noted that *Rocket*'s boiler evaporated 185 gallons water to steam per hour, while modern authors suggest 1,190 lbs of steam per hour, more than enough to meet the demand of the cylinders (118 lbs of steam per mile). John Rastrick noted Rocket's tender carried 300 gallons (1,363 litres) of water, which was topped up during its trial run with 35 gallons; only 30 gallons remained in the tank at the end of the day's experiments, suggesting *Rocket* had evaporated 286 gallons (1,300 litres) – or just under 4 gallons per mile – running the prescribed 70 miles.

Sans Pareil had a total heating surface of 176.7 square feet (53.8 m^2). According to Wood's criteria, her boiler theoretically would have been able to evaporate 3,520 lbs of steam per hour (considerably more than *Rocket*) and have been able to sustain a power output of 14.7 hp. John Rastrick, however, concluded that *Sans Pareil*'s maximum power output in practice was only 10.8 hp (5.4 hp per cylinder) at 50 psi and 10 mph. The lack of a proper firebox prevented a good depth of flame and the fireman would have to frequently push the burning coals forward into the tube, and rake out the ashes and cinders from under the fire bars so that they did not impede the flow of primary air through the fire. Unlike *Rocket*, the gas velocity through the U-shaped flue tube of *Sans Pareil* would have been slow, leading to poor useful heat transfer, despite the 'wetted area' for heat transfer being much larger than *Rocket*. In other words, because *Rocket*'s boiler had twenty-five tubes running through it, the hot gasses were moving at a higher speed as they passed through the boiler and were able to do more useful work before they cooled down than those passing through the U-shaped boiler tube of *Sans Pareil*. *Rocket* would therefore have had a higher exhaust temperature and the gasses at the chimney would have been moving faster and at a higher pressure than with *Sans Pareil*: it is no wonder that *Sans Pareil* needed such a fierce blast-pipe to encourage the flow of gasses through the boiler. Data collected from the 2010

Rocket at rest beneath a brooding Mancunian sky. (David Boydell)

replica *Rocket* shows that the gasses leaving the twenty-five boiler tubes had not given up all their energy, resulting in scorch marks and burning on the base of the chimney. In order to extract the maximum amount of heat, the next generation of Stephenson boilers had eighty-eight tubes, of 2-inch diameter, thus increasing the heating surface, enabling better heat transfer from the gasses to the water in the boiler, and with a lower fuel charge.

We know *Sans Pareil* was certainly capable of making steam, as her water consumption was far higher than *Rocket*: Rastrick indicates that *Rocket* used 286 gallons for a full 70-mile round trip while *Sans Pareil* used 274 gallons, or nearly 10 gallons per mile, to cover half that distance. Rastrick estimated for a full 35-mile journey from Liverpool to Manchester, *Sans Pareil* would have needed 348 gallons of water. That *Sans Pareil* was using nearly twice as much water per mile as *Rocket* indicates that there was something seriously wrong with the locomotive. Davidson and Glitheroe concluded in 2006 that this excessive water consumption indicates the validity of the claim that *Sans Pareil* had a cracked cylinder. They wrote: 'The cylinder must have been cracked, since it was impossible for the locomotive to have used … the amount of water without significant steam leakage.' (Davidson & Glitheroe: 289)

Sans Pareil impatiently blows off at Liverpool Road in 2005. (David Boydell)

Fuel Consumption

The design of boiler and firebox meant that *Rocket* was fuel-efficient: not only in terms of heat transfer (from the twenty-five boiler tubes), but in allowing a good depth of fire and with sufficient space for flame to develop, and therefore flame temperature. On the first day of the Rainhill Trials she burned 1,172 lbs (531 kg) of coke, which Rastrick calculated to be 1,085 lbs (492 kg) per 70-mile round trip on the Liverpool & Manchester. A French observer calculated that *Rocket* burned 147.5 kgs of coke per hour. Thus, *Rocket* was burning 15.5 lbs (7 kg) of coke per mile or 2.31 lbs (*c.* 1 kg) of coke per ton per mile.

Novelty's firebox shared similar features with that of *Rocket*: there was sufficient space for combustion and optimum flame development, as well as a large wetted surface relative to the grate area. Heat transfer via the firebox but also the flue tube was optimised through a high gas velocity (as with *Rocket*) and the small diameter flue tube, as with those of *Rocket*, gave excellent heat transfer. There is no doubt that Briathwaite and Ericsson had designed an excellent boiler.

The firebox of *Sans Pareil* was merely an extension of the main flue, with fire bars 5 feet long. It did not allow for a good depth of fire and gave little space for flame development, therefore giving a lower flame temperature than *Rocket*. The small area in direct contact with the fire (the saddle-shaped water jacket) resulted in poor heat transfer. As a result,

Sans Pareil is recorded as using on average 10 lbs (4.5 kg) of coke per mile more than *Rocket*. This high fuel consumption was due to the poor thermal design of the boiler, and due to the cracked cylinder putting a higher demand on the boiler for steam. The boiler was already handicapped through poor design without having the additional stress of maintaining boiler pressure lost through a leaking cylinder. Because *Sans Pareil* at the 2002 re-enactment of the Rainhill Trials struggled to raise steam and maintain boiler pressure:

> The determination of the crew that, if they could go fast enough, that engine would make as much steam as it used ... full-throttle dashes between marker posts, followed by sometimes lengthy periods stationary to recover steam pressure. [Davidson & Glitheroe: 290]

'The validity of this approach' was borne out through the analysis of *Sans Pareil*'s boiler performance, which suggests that it was incapable of supplying sufficient steam to meet demand at speeds up to 20 mph, but extrapolation of this data suggests the boiler could match steam consumption at 23 mph – in fact the replica managed to achieve a maximum speed of 29 mph with an average speed of 26 mph.

Rocket and *Planet* together in Manchester, 2010. The rapid evolution of the locomotive after Rainhill is shown by the fact that just over twelve months separated the two designs. (Matthew Jackson)

Why *Rocket* Won

Of the three serious contenders entered on 6 October 1829, only *Rocket* was still standing: *Perseverence* and *Cycloped* were obvious false starts. *Sans Pareil* and *Novelty* had both been withdrawn due to mechanical faults – leaking boilers, faulty water pumps and collapsed flue tubes. Of these three, *Novelty* was the most efficient (at 1 per cent) but, as Davidson & Glitheroe note, impractical because it was difficult to fire, and 'prone to tube and grate blockage'.

Novelty, like all forced-air blast locomotives, was hamstrung through using most of her power to work the bellows. Davidson and Glitheroe (2006) concluded that even if the mechanical failures had not occurred, the use of a forced blast from bellows 'significantly undermined the useful output and efficiency' of the locomotive, and therefore the amount of useful work it could perform.

Sans Pareil, despite having a large heating surface, had poor heat transfer characteristics, leading to a poor ability to raise steam and maintain full boiler pressure. Even taking into account the probable burst cylinder, *Sans Pareil*'s boiler design meant that it was unable to meet demand placed upon it. While *Novelty* was able to achieve a higher line speed, it lacked power, or as George Stephenson reputedly put it, 'she's got nay guts'.

A working replica of *Rocket* was built by Robert Stephenson & Co. in 1929 for the American industrialist Henry Ford and is seen in steam with the men who built her.

Rocket's boiler and firebox design was an efficient and economical steam generator able to meet the demand of the cylinders, making her an effective locomotive and, of the three, 'the only one capable of running to a worthwhile timetable'. It was Henry Booth's revolutionary application of the multi-tubular boiler to the locomotive that 'was the reason why ... *Rocket* was the only engine of the three to complete the full seventy-mile course'.

A century of progress 1829–1929: an LNER press photograph of *Rocket* standing in front of a new A3 Class Pacific.

Bibliography

Primary

Manuscript

National Railway Museum, York (NRM):
NRM 1945-108 John Urpeth Rastrick MSS, Rainhill Trials Notebook.
HACK 1-1-10, Hackworth MSS, T. Hackworth to R. Stephenson 7 July 1828.
HACK 1-1-17 Hackworth MSS, J. Rastrick to Hackworth, 3 February 1829.
HACK 1-1-22 Hackworth MSS, T. Hackworth to G. Stephenson, ND.
HACK 1-1-25 Hackworth MSS, T. Hackworth to Liverpool & Manchester Directors, ND.
STESI Correspondence from Robert Stephenson to Samuel Smiles (1854-1858).
STESI/2 Essay by Robert Stephenson on the construction of the Rocket locomotive (1854-1858).

Northumberland Record Office (NRO), Woodhorn:
NRO 602/15 Nicholas Wood Mss, Rainhill Trials Notebook.

The Science Museum, London:
Report on the Competition on the Liverpool and Manchester Railroad.

The National Archives, Kew, London (NA):
RAIL 371/1, Liverpool & Manchester Railway, Mss., Minutes, Board Meetings 1826-1830.
RAIL 371/2, Minutes, Board Meetings, 1830–1833.
RAIL 1008/88/1 Liverpool & Manchester Railway, motive power: reports of George and Robert Stephenson, 1828–1829.
RAIL 1088/88/4 Letters from R. Stephenson to H. Booth dated 3 August 1829, 21 August 1829, 26 August 1829, 31 August 1829, 5 September 1829.

Books
Descriptions des Locomotives Stephenson Circulant sur les chemins de fer en Angleterre et en France (Bruxelles: J-B Champon, 1835).
Booth, H., *An Account of the Liverpool & Manchester Railway* (Liverpool, 1830).

Clark, D. K., *Railway Machinery* (London: Blackie & Son, 1851), 2 vols.

Coste, L., and A. Perdonnet, *Mémoire sur les Chemins À Ornières* (Paris: Bachelier, 1830).

Hebert, L., *History and Progress of the Steam Engine* (London: Thomas Kelly, 1831).

Lobet, J., *Des chemins de fer en France, ou, Traité des principes appliqués à leur tracé, à leur construction et à leur exploitation* (Paris: Parent-Debarres, 1845).

Stephenson, R., and J. Locke, *Observations on the Comparative Merits of Locomotive and Fixed Engines* (Liverpool: Wales & Baines, 1830).

Walker, J., and J. U. P. Rastrick, *Report to the Directors on the Comparative Merits of Loco-Motive and Fixed Engines as a Moving Power* (Liverpool: Wales & Baines, 1829).

Woods, N., *A Practical Treatise on Railroads and interior communication*. Second edition (London: Longman, Orme, Brown, Green & Longmans, 1832).

Journals

Annales des Ponts et Chaussées. Memoires et Documents, 1e serie, 2e semestre, 1831.
Arcana of Science and Art for 1829, 1830.
Mechanics' Magazine, No. 322, 10 October 1829.
Mechanics' Magazine, No. 323, 17 October 1829.
Mechanics' Magazine, No. 324, 24 October 1829.
Mechanics' Magazine, No. 325, 31 October 1829.
Mechanics' Magazine, No. 326, 7 November 1829.
Mechanics' Magazine, No. 327, 14 November 1829.
Mechanics' Magazine, No. 365, 7 August 1830.
Mechanics' Magazine, No. 373, 2 October 1830.
Mechanics' Magazine, No. 375, 16 October 1830.
Mechanics' Magazine, No. 378, 6 November 1830.
Mechanics' Magazine, No. 389, 22 January 1831.
Mechanics' Magazine, No. 397, 19 March 1831.
Register of Arts and Journal of Patent Inventions, Vol. IV, 1830.
Register of Arts and Journal of Patent Inventions, Vol. VI, 1832.
Revue Britannique, Vol. 29, Mars 1830.
The London Journal of Arts and Sciences, Vol. III, 1834.
The Repertory of Patent Inventions, No. LIII, November 1829.

Newspapers

Chester Chronicle
Chester Courant
Leeds Intelligencer
Leeds Mercury
Liverpool Advertiser
Liverpool Mercury
Manchester Courier
Manchester Examiner and Times
Manchester Guardian
Manchester Mercury
The Times

Secondary

Books and Papers

Addyman, J., and V. Howarth (eds.), *Robert Stephenson: Railway Engineer* (North Eastern Railway Association, 2005).

Ahrons, E. L., *The British Steam Railway Locomotive 1825–1925* (London: Locomotive Publishing Co. Ltd, 1927).

Bailey, M. R., 'Robert Stephenson & Co. 1823–1829' in *Transactions of the Newcomen Society*, vol. 50, (1979–1980), pp. 252–291.

Bailey, M. R., 'George Stephenson – Locomotive Advocate' in *Transactions of the Newcomen Society*, vol. 52 (1980–1981), pp. 171–207.

Bailey, M. R., 'Leaning Through Replication: The Planet Project' in *Transactions of the Newcomen Society*, vol. 68 (1996–1997), pp. 109–136.

Bailey, M. R., and J. P. Glitheroe, *The Engineering and History of Rocket* (London: The Science Museum, 2000).

Bailey, M. R. (ed.), *Robert Stephenson – The Eminent Engineer* (London: Routledge, 2003).

Bailey, M. R., 'Restaging the Rainhill Trials. Learning through replication' in M. R. Bailey (ed.), *Early Railways* 3 (Sudbury: Six Martlets, 2006), pp. 270–271.

Davidson, P., and J. P. Glitheroe, 'Analysis of Locomotive Performance', in M. R. Bailey (ed.), *Early Railways* 3 (Sudbury: Six Martlets, 2006), pp. 284–299.

Dendy Marshall, C. F., *A History of Railway Locomotives down to the end of the year 1831* (London: Locomotive Publishing Co. Ltd., 1953).

King, W. T., *History of the American Steam Fire Engine* (Boston: Pinkham Press, 1896).

Lamb, R., 'Something of a Novelty', in M. R. Bailey (ed.), *Early Railways* 3 (Sudbury: Six Martlets, 2006), pp. 272–283.

Satow, F., M. G. Satow and L. S. Wilson, *Locomotion: Concept to Creation. The story of the reproduction 1973–1975* (Locomotion Trust: Beamish, 1976).

Smiles, R., *Memoir of Henry Booth* (London: Wyman & Sons, 1869).

Smiles, S., *Lives of the Engineers*, Vol. III (London: John Murray, 1862).

Snell, J. B., *Railways: Mechanical Engineering* (London: The Longman Group Ltd., 1971).

Warren, J. G. H., *A Century of Locomotive Building by Robert Stephenson & Co., 1823–1923* (Newcastle upon Tyne: Andrew Reid & Co., 1923).

Wilson, R., *A Treatise on Steam Boilers* (London: Lockwood & Co., 1873).

Young, C. F. T., *Fires, Fire Engines, and Fire Brigades, with a History of Manual and Steam Fire Engines* (London: Lockwood, 1866).

Young, R., *Timothy Hackworth and the Locomotive*, third edition (Lewes: The Book Guild Ltd., 2000).

Printed and bound by CPI Group (UK) Ltd, Croydon, CR0 4YY